Skill Sharpeners 4

SECOND EDITION

Judy DeFilippo
Charles Skidmore

ADDISON-WESLEY PUBLISHING COMPANY

Reading, Massachusetts • Menlo Park, California
New York • Don Mills, Ontario • Wokingham, England
Amsterdam • Bonn • Sydney • Singapore • Tokyo • Madrid • San Juan

Judy DeFilippo is a coordinator of ESL in the Intensive English program at Northeastern University. She is author of *Lifeskills 1* and *2* and *Lifeskills and Citizenship*, and is co-author of *Grammar Plus*, all published by Addison-Wesley.

Charles Skidmore is an ESL teacher at the secondary level in the Boston, Massachusetts, schools and at Boston University's CELOP program. He is co-author of *In Good Company* also published by Addison-Wesley.

A Publication of the World Language Division

Editorial: Talbot Hamlin, Elly Schottman

Production/Manufacturing: James W. Gibbons

Illustrations: Kathleen Todd, Walter Fournier

Cover design: Marshall Henrichs, Richard Hannus

Photographs:
Page 10: National Aeronautics and Space Administration
Page 108: Boston Globe Photo by John Tlumacki

ISBN 0-201-51328-5

5 6 7 8 9 10 PO 96 95

Introduction

The *Skill Sharpeners* series has been especially designed for students whose skills in standard English, especially those skills concerned with reading and writing, require strengthening. It is directed both toward students whose first language is not English and toward those who need additional practice in standard English grammar and vocabulary. By introducing basic skills tied to classroom subjects in a simple, easy-to-understand grammatical framework, the series helps to prepare these students for success in regular ("mainstream") academic subjects. By developing and reinforcing school and life survival skills, it helps build student confidence and self esteem.

This second edition of *Skill Sharpeners* not only updates the content of many pages, it also provides increased focus for some of the grammar exercises and adds new emphasis on higher order thinking skills. In addition, there are more content-area readings, more biographies, new opportunities for students to write, and more practice in using formats similar to those of many standardized tests. The central purpose of the series remains the same, however. *Skill Sharpeners* remains dedicated to helping your students sharpen their skills in all facets of English communication.

With English as a Second Language students, *Skill Sharpeners* supplements and complements any basic ESL text or series. With these students and with others, *Skill Sharpeners* can also be used to reteach and reinforce specific skills with which students are having—or have had—difficulty. In addition, it can be used to review and practice grammatical structures and to reinforce, expand, and enrich students' vocabularies.

The grammatical structures in the *Skill Sharpeners* series follow a systematic, small-step progression with many opportunities for practice, review, and reinforcement. Vocabulary and skill instruction is presented in the context of situations and concepts that have an immediate impact on students' daily lives. Themes and subject matter are directly related to curriculum areas. Reading and study skills are stressed in many pages, and writing skills are carefully developed, starting with single words and sentences and building gradually to paragraphs and stories in a structured, controlled composition sequence.

If you are using *Skill Sharpeners* with a basic text or series, you may find that the structural presentation in *Skill Sharpeners* deviates from that in your text. In such a case, you should not expect most of your students to be able actively to use the structures on some pages in speaking or writing. The students should, however, be able to read and respond to the content. Do not be concerned about structural errors during discussion of the material. It is important that students become *actively involved* and *communicating*, however imperfectly, from the very beginning.

Using the *Skill Sharpeners*

Because each page or pair of pages of the *Skill Sharpeners* books is independent and self contained, the series lends itself to great flexibility of use. Teachers may pick and choose pages that fit the needs of particular students, or they may use the pages in sequential order. Most pages are self-explanatory, and all are easy to use, either in class or as homework assignments. Annotations at the bottom of each page identify the skill or skills being developed and suggest ways to prepare for, introduce, and present the exercise(s) on the page. In most cases, oral practice of the material is suggested before the student is asked to complete the page in writing. Teacher demonstration and student involvement and participation help build a foundation for completing the page successfully and learning the skill.

The *Skill Sharpeners* are divided into thematic units. The first unit of each book is introductory. In *Skill Sharpeners 1*, this unit provides exercises to help students say and write their names and addresses and to familiarize them with basic classroom language, school deportment, the names of school areas and school personnel, and number names. In later books of the series, the first unit serves both to review some of the material taught in earlier books and to provide orientation to the series for students coming to it for the first time.

At the end of each of the *Skill Sharpeners* books is a review of vocabulary and an end-of-book test of grammatical and reading skills. The test, largely in multiple-choice format, not only assesses learning of the skills but also provides additional practice for other multiple-choice tests.

The complete Table of Contents in each book identifies the skills developed on each page. A Skills Index at the end of the book lists skills alphabetically by topic and indicates the pages on which they are developed.

Skill Sharpeners invite expansion! We encourage you to use them as a springboard and to add activities and exercises that build on those in the books to fill the needs of your own particular students. Used this way, the *Skill Sharpeners* can significantly help to build the confidence and skills that students need to be successful members of the community and successful achievers in subject-area classrooms.

Contents

5

UNIT 4   It's Up to You, Isn't It?

UNIT 5   Wheels

UNIT 6   How Do You Say It?

UNIT 7 Decisions, Decisions

UNIT 8 Be a Good Sport

UNIT 9 On the Job

Getting to Know You

Interview as many classmates as you can to get "Yes" answers to the questions below. Try to get more than one "Yes" answer to each question. Write the name of each student who answers "Yes" to a question on the line after the question, along with any other information needed. Be ready to share your answers with the class.

1. Will you have a birthday soon? When? _____

2. Can you name five U.S. Presidents? Who? _____

   _____

3. Would you like to be an astronaut someday? _____

4. Can you name the capital of El Salvador? What is it? _____

5. Do you have three sisters and a brother? _____

6. Are you the oldest in your family? _____

7. Would you like to be a surgeon? _____

8. Can you play a musical instrument? What? _____

9. Can you play tennis or handball? _____

10. Have you ever kissed a dog or a cat? _____

11. Do you have a part time job? What is it? _____

12. Have you ridden in a taxi recently? Where did you go? _____

13. Do you like to watch baseball on TV? _____

14. Have you ever swallowed a fly? _____

15. Have you ever acted in a play? _____

16. Did you ever ride on a rollercoaster? _____

17. Have you ever walked in your sleep? _____

18. Have you ever given a speech to a group? _____

Skill Objectives: Interviewing; making an oral report. Ask the class if anyone had a birthday within the past week (month, three months). When was it? Draw a line on the board and write the person's name and the date. Ask other questions (motor boat ride, trip to another city, etc.) and record names and details. Tell students they are going to ask similar questions (those on the page) to classmates; they are to try to get at least one "yes" answer to each question. Students are to record their answers, then report to the class.

9

Complete the Sentence

A. Complete each sentence by filling the blank with one word or more than one word that makes sense. Make sure your sentences are correct grammatically.

Example: People here __*are / seem / act / aren't*__ friendly.

(Any of the answers filled in above would be correct. You may be able to think of others, too.)

1. Every day the children _____ .

2. John drives carefully, but his brother _____ .

3. Right now she _____ in the kitchen.

4. The teacher always _____ .

5. He _____ a week ago.

6. She is _____ than he is.

7. In 1987, we _____ .

8. Next year we _____ .

9. This is the most _____ of them all.

10. Since 1989 he _____ .

11. I had an accident while I _____ .

12. She has never _____ .

13. Carlos wasn't at the game but his brothers _____ .

14. She said _____ .

B. Fill in each blank space with one word. Be sure your words make sense and are correct grammatically. The first one is done for you.

In July, 1969, astronauts Neil Armstrong and Edwin Aldrin landed ____*on*____ the moon. They walked, collected rocks, _____ put an American flag there.

Two _____ later, in July, 1971, astronauts David Scott and Charles Irwin _____ to the moon and brought with them _____ special "car," a Moon Rover. They _____ the car for five miles. The top speed _____ seven miles per hour.

"Man, oh Man!" cried Scott.

"What a Grand Prix" this is.

Skill Objectives: Reviewing grammar; completing a cloze exercise. At the beginning of the course, it is important to find out what grammatical structures your English students have not previously learned. This exercise gives you a fast, useful overview. *Part A:* Tell students to write one or more words that will complete each sentence. Do the example on the board together and ask for other words that might complete it (*appear to be, look, are never,* etc.). Give students as much time as they need. *Part B:* After explaining directions carefully on the board, you may assign this as written work for individuals or pairs. When students have completed it, discuss all possible responses, explaining why some are correct and some are not.

Whose Are They?

In English, you can often say the same thing in several different ways. Look at the examples below:

The book belongs to Jack.　　　　The coat belongs to me.
It's Jack's book.　　　　　　　　It's my coat.
It's his book.　　　　　　　　　　It's mine.
It's his.

"Jack's" is a possessive noun. To form the possessive of a singular noun, you add an apostrophe (') and *s*. To form the possessive of a regular plural noun, you just add an apostrophe *(boys')*. For a plural noun that does not end in *s* or *es (men, oxen)* you add *'s (men's, oxen's)*.

"His" is a possessive adjective. There are two kinds: *my, your, his, her, its, our, their;* and *mine, yours, his, hers, ours, theirs.* The first group is used with a noun *(It's their book).* The second group is used without a noun *(It's theirs).*

Read each of the sentences below. Then rewrite each one in different ways, using the example above as a model. The first one is done for you.

1. The ball belongs to Mary.
   It's Mary's ball.
   It's her ball.
   It's hers.

2. These coats belong to the Rays.
   _____
   _____
   _____

3. These dogs belong to James.
   _____
   _____
   _____

4. The calculator belongs to me.
   _____
   _____

5. The games belong to us.
   _____
   _____

6. The cats belong to you.
   _____
   _____

7. The tape belongs to Ann.
   _____
   _____
   _____

8. The hat belongs to Ed.
   _____
   _____
   _____

9. These boots belong to Pam.
   _____
   _____
   _____

10. That bat belongs to you.
    _____
    _____

11. Those glasses belong to us.
    _____
    _____

12. The pen belongs to me.
    _____
    _____

Skill Objectives: Forming and using possessive nouns and adjectives; restating ideas in different ways. Review/teach the formation of possessives. Draw attention to the two uses of the apostrophe. Work through the examples with the class, and show how the first item follows them. Do some or all of the remaining items orally with the class before assigning as written work.

11

Long, Longer, Longest

A. Place the correct form of the adjective in each sentence. Be careful of spelling changes in some of the words. Use *er* or *est* for short words and *more* and *the most* for longer words. The first two are done for you.

1. The Nile is _____*the longest*_____ (long) river in the world.

2. Alaska is _____*larger*_____ (large) than Texas.

3. Los Angeles is _____ (big) than Boston.

4. In 1910, England was _____ (powerful) nation in the world.

5. A Mercedes is _____ (expensive) than a Volkswagen.

6. Florida has _____ (long) coastline of all the fifty states.

7. The climate of New York is _____ (cold) than that of Miami.

8. Mount Everest is _____ (high) mountain in the world.

9. Gold is _____ (valuable) than silver.

10. Saint Augustine is _____ (old) city in the United States.

B. Use the correct form of *good* or *bad* in these sentences. (Use *a* or *the* with your adjectives if you need to.) The first one is done for you.

1. Fruit is _____*better*_____ (good) for you than candy.

2. Many people think February is _____ (bad) month of the year.

3. Jorge feels _____ (bad) today than he did yesterday.

4. Carla speaks English _____ (good) than she writes it.

5. Lincoln was President during _____ (bad) period in history.

6. The pollution in Los Angeles is _____ (bad) than the pollution in New York City.

7. The San Francisco earthquake of 1906 was _____ (bad) earthquake disaster in the history of California.

8. *Gandhi* was voted _____ (good) movie of 1982.

9. Many educators believe that Harvard University is _____ (good) university in the world.

10. Route 95 is _____ (good) highway from New York to Washington than it is from Boston to New York.

C. Choose appropriate adjectives to complete these sentences. Be sure your adjective makes sense in the sentence and that it is in the correct form. (Use *a* or *the* with your adjectives if you need to.)

1. Juan thought Maria was _____ girl in the world!

2. Richard has _____ stereo system than Ramona does.

3. The Cadillac is _____ automobile.

4. Television is _____ invention of the past 60 years.

5. New York is _____ state than Iowa.

Skill Objectives: Forming and using comparatives and superlatives, including those of *good*; using vocabulary in context. Teach/review the rules for forming comparatives and superlatives. Do Part A orally; have volunteers explain their answers. Discuss the comparative and superlative forms of *good*, then assign the page as written work.

Cars and Houses

> 1. "The same" + a noun is one way to express a similarity.
>   Example: Susan and Fred are *the same age.*
> 2. "The same as" is also used to express a similarity.
>   Example: Susan's car is the same as John's car.
>   or: Susan's car is *the same color as* John's car.

Cars are expensive, but houses are much more expensive! Mary and Susan know this, because each of them owns a car and a house.

A. Look at the information about their cars.

Nouns	Mary's Car	Susan's Car
Color:	Blue	Blue
Make:	Chevrolet	Chevrolet
Model:	Station Wagon	Sedan
Year:	1989	1986
Price:	$14,000	$9,500

Write some sentences comparing the two cars. The first two are done for you. Use them as models.

1. *Mary's car is the same color as Susan's car.* _____
2. *Mary's car is* _____
3. _____
4. _____
5. _____

B. Now look at information about their houses.

Nouns	Mary's House	Susan's House
Value:	$210,000	$360,000
Age:	40 Years Old	10 Years Old
Style:	Colonial	Modern
Color:	White	White
Size:	7 Rooms	10 Rooms

On your own paper, write some sentences comparing the two houses. Use *nouns* such as value, age, style, color or size. Or you can use *adjectives* such as old, modern, large, or expensive.

C. Write a short composition comparing different schools you have attended.

Skill Objectives: Using comparatives; interpreting data. Discuss with students that cars and houses are the two most expensive purchases that many people make. Call attention to the data on the cars, and have volunteers read the first two sentences. Do the rest of Part A orally. Discuss the information on the houses and do two sentences orally. Then assign the entire page as written work.

13

That's Superlative!

A. Change each of the adjectives in the phrases at the left into its superlative form, and then use the phrase in a sentence of your own. The first one is done for you.

big city 1. _New York is the biggest city in our country._

famous actress 2. _____

good singer 3. _____

cold state 4. _____

hot state 5. _____

tall building 6. _____

interesting personality 7. _____

good movie 8. _____

B. Now write sentences that use the phrase *one of the* followed by a superlative. For example, "Boston is *one of the oldest* cities in the United States." Or, "Boston is *one of the most polluted* cities in the United States." Use the phrases in the box to make your sentences.

large state	rich man	good university
long river	small state	famous movie star
beautiful city	important writer	talented rock group
popular tourist attraction		

1. _____
2. _____
3. _____
4. _____
5. _____
6. _____
7. _____
8. _____
9. _____
10. _____

C. On your paper, write a paragraph about your country. Use the phrases in the box above if you wish, or any of the following, or both. Use superlatives in your paragraph.

big city	famous athlete	good artist
important industry	beautiful view	popular musician

Skill Objectives: Forming and using superlatives; writing descriptive paragraphs. *Part A:* Review the two ways of forming superlatives (with the ending *est* and with the word *most*). Have a volunteer tell why "big city" is changed to "the biggest city" in Item 1. Do the remaining items orally, then assign as written work. *Part B:* Do several sentences orally, then assign as written work. Part C may be used as a homework assignment.

Similes

A. A simile (SIM-uh-lee) is a way of describing something by comparing it to something else. Good writers use interesting, vivid similes to help readers form pictures in their minds. Some similes are used over and over, however. Like old bread or cake, they become stale. It is important to know them, just the same, because you will hear and see them so often. The similes in Column Y are often used in conversation. **Match them with the sentence beginnings in Column X by writing the letter of the simile in the blank that follows the sentence beginning.**

X

1. Your hands are freezing; they're _____

2. It's easy to pick up the baby; he's _____

3. My brother never makes any noise, he's _____

4. Hurry, Juan! You're _____

5. Professor Collins's class is awfully dull. It's _____

6. The gun shot rang out in the night. It was _____

7. Our new house is huge; it's _____

8. Paul would never hurt anybody; he's _____

9. His girlfriend is lovely; she's _____

10. Sandy can't lift the box; it's _____

11. Look at the sheets and pillowcases; they're _____

12. Raoul's eyes shine; they're _____

13. Everybody knows that ancient joke; it's _____

14. Children like this medicine; it's _____

15. Myra is very cheerful today; she's _____

Y

a. as big as a castle.
b. as loud as thunder.
c. as pretty as a picture.
d. as boring as yesterday's news.
e. as white as snow.
f. as bright as stars.
g. as old as the hills.
h. as sweet as sugar.
i. as cold as ice.
j. as gentle as a lamb.
k. as light as a feather.
l. as quiet as a mouse.
m. as happy as a lark.
n. as heavy as lead.
o. as slow as a turtle.

B. Now make up similes of your own. Be fresh and inventive! Some sentence beginnings are given, to get you started. Write your own for the other similes.

1. Alana's room was as colorful as _____

2. The night was as dark as _____

3. Paul's face was as red as _____

4. Luis is as stubborn as _____

5. The students were as curious as _____

6. _____

7. _____

8. _____

9. _____

10. _____

Skill Objective: Understanding and creating similes. *Part A:* Discuss the definition of a simile at the top of the page. Elicit that similes are used to help hearers or readers to understand better what we are trying to communicate. Do the first three items orally, and discuss how the similes accomplish this purpose. Assign as written work. *Part B:* Stress the creation of fresh, inventive similes. Ask several students to provide different answers for the first three items, then assign as written work.

15

Reading the Newspaper:
The Index

Every large city has at least one daily newspaper. Many small cities and towns also have daily newspapers. Your daily newspaper is an important source of information. Television can give you some of the news, but a newspaper can give you more. It can "cover" (provide information about) your own area—your city or town, your country, and your state, and give you information about the rest of the world as well. It can tell you about sales in stores near you, about programs on your television channels, and about movies in your theaters. It can keep you up to date on your own sports teams, and on major professional teams all over the nation. It can help you find a place to live, a car to buy, and a job. Get to know your newspaper! To help you, each unit in this book has pages on Reading the Newspaper. These will help you find out about some of the features in your own daily paper.

Most newspapers have an index. Just as the Table of Contents in a book tells you where to find each chapter, the Index in a newspaper tells you where to find different kinds of information. Look at the Index below. Notice that here it has a different name. In your paper it may be called something else.

Guide to Features

Arts/Films	24	Horoscope	43
Bridge	43	Living Section	27
Business	13	Obituaries	38, 39
Classified	43–62	Sports	31
Comics	46	TV and Radio	41
Editorials	16	Weather	10

A. Match the names of the sections at the left with the kind of information that is found in them at the right by writing the right letter in each blank. The first one is done for you.

1. Arts/Films __d__

2. Bridge ____

3. Business ____

4. Classified ____

5. Comics ____

6. Editorials ____

7. Horoscope ____

8. Living Section ____

9. Obituaries ____

10. Sports ____

11. TV and Radio ____

12. Weather ____

a. news of the stock market, banks, and companies

b. lists of programs seen and heard in the area

c. the cartoon page

d. news of movies, theater, art exhibits, concerts

e. meteorological forecasts, temperature, etc.

f. ads for jobs, cars, houses, apartments

g. opinions of newspaper owners, staff, and readers

h. reports of baseball, football, hockey games

i. recipes, interior decorating, etiquette, advice

j. fun column for "fortune telling"

k. list of persons who have died recently

l. suggestions for playing a popular card game

Skill Objectives: Classifying; identifying main idea; using an index; learning about newspapers. Ask how many students read a daily newspaper regularly. What can a newspaper give them that television and radio cannot? What kinds of things can one find in a newspaper? Tell students that each unit in this book will have material on the newspaper and its parts. Then discuss the use of the newspaper's index or table of contents. *Part A:* Do the first several items orally, then assign for written work.

16

B. Use the Index on the preceding page to answer the following questions. The first one is done for you.

1. On what page would you find a story about the spring fashion shows in Paris and New York? __27__

2. Where would you look to find out about a movie that opened last night? _____

3. You're thinking about buying a used car. Where will you look in the paper? _____

4. On what page will you probably find an article about a merger of two large corporations? _____

5. You're a Taurus. Where do you look to find out what your day is supposed to be like? _____

6. Your friend's grandmother just died. Where will you look to find out when her funeral is going to be? _____

7. Your city is going to elect a new mayor soon. Where do you look to find out which candidate the newspaper management is backing? _____

8. You'd like to go on a picnic tomorrow. Where will you look to see if this is a good idea or not? _____

9. You like to play cards, but sometimes you don't know what to bid. Where can you look for suggestions? _____

10. Where will you look to find out what Charlie Brown and Snoopy are up to today? _____

11. Your friend has said that there are reruns of M*A*S*H on every day. Where will you look to see when they are on? _____

12. Your school track team is in a big meet with teams from other schools in your state. Where will you look to find out how well they succeeded yesterday? _____

C. The Index on the preceding page tells you where to find some kinds of news—news about business, sports, or cultural events, for example. But it does not tell you where to find general news—news about what's happening in the Middle East or Europe or Central America, for example, or news about what the different candidates for mayor said yesterday. **Think of some headings you might add to a Table of Contents to show people where to find different kinds of news.** One is done for you.

National News _____   _____

_____   _____

_____   _____

D. Get a copy of your local daily newspaper. Attach the Index to the top of a sheet of paper. Then list at least one piece of information you found in each section of the paper mentioned in the Table of Contents.

Skill Objectives: Classifying; identifying main idea; using a newspaper index; interpreting section headings. *Part B:* Do the first three questions orally, then assign as written work. *Part C:* Discuss possible additional headings before assigning as written work. Part D may be assigned as homework.

Whose Is It?

There are five mailboxes in the local post office in Boxford. The five boxes belong to five people in the town. During months of sorting mail, the postal worker has guessed certain facts about these five people. Using the fourteen pieces of information below as clues, you should be able to figure out which mailbox belongs to whom, and the occupation of each mailbox holder.

1. Richard Brady is an insurance salesman.

2. The owner of Box 3 is an electrician.

3. The banker uses an end box.

4. The teacher's name is Mr. Mahoney.

5. The box before the electrician's box belongs to Ms. Donley.

6. Frank is an electrician.

7. Susan once got Sam's mail in a mix up.

8. Box 1 belongs to the Owen family.

9. Jennifer uses Box 2.

10. The insurance salesman is next to the teacher.

11. The accountant uses Box 2.

12. The insurance salesman uses Box 5.

13. The Adlers' box is not next to the insurance salesman's box.

14. Sam's mailbox is next to Frank's.

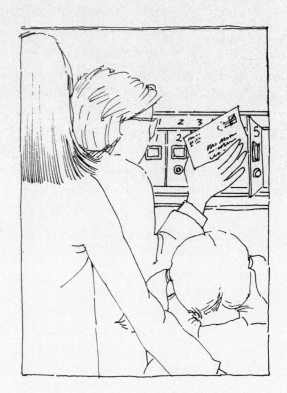

Now, fill in the names and occupations of the box holders. You will have to read through the clues several times. Good luck!

	First Name	Last Name	Occupation
Box 1			
Box 2			
Box 3			
Box 4			
Box 5			

Skill Objectives: Deductive problem solving; reading for details. Read the instructions, then draw a row of boxes on the board, numbered 1 to 5. Establish that 1 and 5 are the "end boxes." Tell students they are to find out the first and last names and occupations of the five box holders. Suggest that they draw a row of boxes like the one on the board and write clues under them as they discover them. You may wish to have students work in pairs to solve the problem.

Dear Dot

Dear Dot—

What do girls like to do on a date? I'm not talking about going out to eat or to a movie, but before and after that. What do girls like to talk about? When I go to her house, do I have to talk to her parents? What about at the end of the date? Is a kiss on the first date all right? Anything else? I am going to be dating soon, so any information you can give me will be helpful. I don't want to look ridiculous. Thanks.

Bashful

Discuss each of the questions in class. Then write your answer.

1. Do girls and boys usually like to talk about the same things? Why or why not?

_____

_____

2. Does a date usually meet his girlfriend's parents? Why or why not?

_____

_____

3. Is a kiss on the first date all right? Why or why not?

_____

_____

4. Why does the writer sign himself "Bashful"? What does *bashful* mean?

_____

_____

Write About It

Now put yourself in Dot's place. Write a helpful answer to Bashful. Remember, you want to help him solve his problem, not make fun of him or criticize him.

Dear Bashful—

_____

_____

_____

_____

_____

_____

_____

_____

Skill Objectives: Reading for main idea; making inferences; generalizing from experiences; expressing opinions in writing. Read the letter aloud (or have a student read it). Discuss each question in class. Encourage free expression of opinion, but be sure students can support their opinions. Then have students write answers to the questions. Suggest that they use these answers as the basis for their letters. You may wish to assign the letter-writing activity as homework.

19

How Do They Do It?

An adverb is a word that tells *how*. Most adverbs are formed by adding *ly* to an adjective, but some adverbs are irregular. Look at the following list of adjectives and their adverbs.

Adjective	Adverb	Adjective	Adverb	Adjective	Adverb
careful	carefully	quick	quickly	angry	angrily
careless	carelessly	slow	slowly	good	well
polite	politely	impatient	impatiently	fast	fast
beautiful	beautifully	accurate	accurately	hard	hard

A. Change the adjectives to adverbs to answer the questions. Use your dictionary if you need to. The first one is done for you.

1. Tom is a careful driver.
   How does he drive?   *He drives carefully.*

2. Susan is a beautiful dancer.
   How does she dance?   _____

3. Ed and John are terrible singers.
   How do they sing?   _____

4. My father is a dangerous driver.
   How does he drive?   _____

5. Carolina is a fast typist.
   How does she type?   _____

6. Carlos is a good tennis player.
   How does he play?   _____

B. Look at the list that shows the comparative forms of some adverbs. Use it to complete the sentences. Use each adverb only once.

better than	slower *or* more slowly than	more carefully than
worse than	louder *or* more loudly than	more quickly than
later than	neater *or* more neatly than	more beautifully than
earlier than	easier *or* more easily than	more accurately than

1. John feels _____ today than he did yesterday.

2. Do you speak English _____ than your father does?

3. Do you dress _____ than your friends?

4. Does your mother drive _____ than your father?

5. Lisa works _____ than her sister.

6. Do you go to bed _____ or _____ than your parents?

7. I speak Spanish _____ than I speak English.

8. Do you read _____ than you did a year ago?

9. She does her homework _____ than most students.

10. Marco often talks _____ than he needs to.

Skill Objectives: Forming and using adverbs; using the comparative form of adverbs; using context to complete sentences. Draw attention to the definition of "adverb" and the examples showing how adverbs are formed from adjectives. Ask for other adjectives, write them on the board, and help students form the related adverbs. *Part A:* Do the items orally, then assign as written work. *Part B:* Discuss the two ways of forming comparatives, elicit when each is used, then assign the ten items as written work.

20

How Did They Say It?

Read each sentence. Add an appropriate adverb from the Data Bank to complete it. Although the same adverb might be used in several sentences, you may use each adverb only once, so choose carefully.

1. "My best friend moved away last week," the boy said _____.

2. "I can't wait to get started," Paula said _____.

3. "Help me! Help me! I've been robbed!" the woman cried _____.

4. "Sshh! The baby is sleeping," the young mother said _____.

5. "I don't like to go to parties where I don't know anyone," the girl said

   _____.

6. "Darling, you are the most wonderful daughter that a father ever had," the man said

   _____.

7. "I wish I could buy that horse," said Jill _____.

8. "I'm sorry. I didn't realize that this was a private beach," the woman said

   _____.

9. "I shall never set foot in this restaurant again," the customer shouted

   _____.

10. "Are you sure that you didn't copy Roberto's exam?" the teacher asked

    _____.

11. "Well, you aren't wrong, but you're not exactly right," the counselor explained

    _____.

12. "I hate to go, but I suppose I have to," said Tony _____.

13. "I did it. I stole the five dollars," the boy admitted _____.

14. "Do you think I'll pass my driver's test?" Danny asked _____.

15. "I just can't seem to make it come out right," the student wailed _____.

D A T A B A N K

angrily	anxiously	apologetically	desperately	enthusiastically
helplessly	longingly	lovingly	quietly	reluctantly
sadly	shyly	suspiciously	tactfully	truthfully

Skill Objectives: Using adverbs; building vocabulary; using context to complete sentences. Read the directions with the students. Emphasize both that more than one of the adverbs in the Data Bank may fit in a particular sentence and that the same adverb may fit several sentences; however, the student must use each adverb only once. Students may wish to "try out" answers in the margin. Students should use dictionaries for adverbs that are unfamiliar. You may wish to assign this page as homework.

Summaries

A summary is a short statement of the important information contained in a paragraph, a story, or a longer reading selection. Look at the examples. Then write summaries of the other paragraphs.

Example 1

The Queen Elizabeth II, usually called the QE 2, is a large, modern passenger ship. The QE 2, which is actually an enormous floating hotel, can carry 2,000 passengers. A staff of 950 other people run the ship and take care of the passengers. The ship has three restaurants, four swimming pools, two movie theaters, two libraries, a hospital, and many other facilities. It takes passengers for cruises all over the world.

Summary: *The Queen Elizabeth II, a large ship that can carry 2,000 people, has several restaurants, swimming pools, and other facilities, and is used for world-wide cruises.*

Example 2

Harry Houdini, a magician born in 1874, was famous because of the fantastic things he could do. For example, he could escape from anything. During his career as a performer, Houdini escaped from handcuffs and chains, from straitjackets, from a locked box under water, and from many prisons. But one night in 1926, in front of an audience in a big theater, Houdini couldn't escape. He was upside down in a tank of water, with locks and chains all around the tank. Try as he could, he wasn't able to get out and, in full view of the audience, the Great Houdini drowned.

Summary: *Harry Houdini, a famous magician who could escape from almost anything, died when he was unable to get out of a locked tank of water.*

On your paper, write summaries of the following stories.

Story 1

It was one of the most exciting games of the season. In the first half, the Red Wings made two touchdowns and scored two extra points. In the second half, however, the White Sox made a comeback. "Killer" Kowalski, their quarterback, led them to three winning plays, and the Super Sox won again with a final score of 27 to 14.

Story 2

The Statue of Liberty, on Liberty Island in New York harbor, was a gift of the people of France to the United States. It was designed by a French sculptor, Frederic Auguste Bartholdi, who began work on it in 1874. The statue arrived in America in 214 packing cases and was put together on its granite base on what was then called Bedloe's Island. The last rivet holding together the copper sheets that make up the outside of the statue was driven on October 28, 1886, when President Grover Cleveland dedicated the monument. The statue is 151 feet high, from the base to the tip of the torch. It weighs 225 tons. In 1984 to 1986 the statue was rebuilt. The frame was repaired, the torch was replaced, and an elevator was added. The restored statue was reopened to the public at a celebration on July 4, 1986.

Skill Objectives: Reading for main idea; writing a summary. Read the definition of a summary with the class. Have students look at the two examples. Elicit that the summaries contain the main ideas of the longer passages but omit many of the details. Ask students to write a first draft of a summary of the football game story, and have several of these read and discussed. Then assign the rest of the page. Allow time for students to complete the page, then have them work in pairs, comparing and discussing their summaries.

In a Few Words . . .

Write a brief summary of a full-length article.

On the preceding page you wrote summaries of short paragraphs. More often you will be asked to write summaries of longer stories or articles. **Read the story below on earthquakes in California. Then write a summary of it.**

Just before dawn on April 18, 1906, San Francisco was shaken by a major earthquake. The quake measured 8.3 on the Richter scale. Buildings collapsed, and fires devastated four square miles of the city. At least 450 people lost their lives. On October 17, 1989, San Francisco was struck by another severe earthquake, measuring 7.1 on the Richter scale. Again, buildings collapsed, but this time the fires were controlled. Skyscrapers, all built since the 1906 quake, swayed but stood the shock better than many smaller buildings.

San Francisco was quickly rebuilt after both the 1906 and 1989 earthquakes, but scientists say that another huge earthquake will strike the city some time in the future, and it may be even more powerful than the one in 1906.

There are actually hundreds of earthquakes every day in California. Most are so small that they can be detected only by very sensitive instruments. But some, like those in 1906 and 1989 are much more powerful.

Earthquakes are caused by the movement of 60- to 90-mile-thick plates of rock that make up the crust of the earth. Where two plates meet, there are "faults" in the earth's surface. Forces in the earth put pressure on the plates to move, but friction keeps them from moving. When the pressure gets strong enough, the plates suddenly move against each other. This sudden motion is an earthquake.

The San Andreas Fault, in California, is the boundary between what scientists have called the Pacific plate and the American plate. The San Andreas fault runs generally southeast to northwest, roughly parallel to the California coast. It crosses 650 miles of the California landscape from the Gulf of California in the south to north of San Francisco. Scientists know that the San Andreas Fault has been moving at a rate of two inches a year, gradually tearing a great area of California away from the mainland and into the Pacific.

Los Angeles, only 50 miles from the fault, and San Francisco, right on it, have both grown tremendously since the earthquake of 1906. Both cities are dependent on imported water, complex highway systems, gas pipelines, and underground wires for electricity and telephone. All of these could be disrupted for weeks and even months by a major earthquake. An elevated highway was destroyed with loss of many lives in the 1989 earthquake and one of the bridges across San Francisco Bay was closed for weeks because of damage. Los Angeles escaped the 1989 quake. Next time Los Angeles may not be so lucky.

Write your summary below.

_____
_____
_____
_____
_____
_____
_____
_____
_____
_____

Skill Objectives: Reading for main idea; choosing relevant details; writing a summary. Have the story read. (You may wish to read it aloud to the class or have a student or students do so.) Discuss with the group what ideas should be included in a summary, and write these on the board as they are offered and agreed upon. Suggest that students copy these and use them as they write their summaries. You may wish to assign the writing of the summaries as homework.

Reading the Newspaper: Headlines

A. A headline is the line of large print above a newspaper story. It calls attention to the story and usually gives the main idea. **Read the following stories. Then look at the four headlines in the box below and write each one above the story it goes with.**

_____

_____

A pall of smoke covered downtown Righton yesterday afternoon as a three-alarm fire gutted the Allston Travel Agency at 47 Bagley Street.

It took the several companies at the scene more than four hours to control the fire, which damaged three stores as well as the Agency. No one was injured, but Chief George H. Daniels estimated damage at over $100,000.

The cause of the fire is undetermined. The area surrounding the Agency has been the scene of several fires in recent years. The Fire Marshal's office is investigating.

_____

_____

Mrs. Karen Schultz, of Sunset Lane in Ashburn, celebrated her 99th birthday yesterday by cleaning house and cooking dinner for her son and daughter who are visiting her from Nebraska.

Born in Omaha, Mrs. Schultz lived there most of her life until coming to Ashburn ten years ago. She taught school for many years and says she still enjoys working with neighborhood children who need help with their studies.

Asked for the secret of a long life, the former teacher said "Learn to laugh at your troubles. Laughter is the best medicine."

_____

_____

An unidentified man was pulled from the Harley River late yesterday afternoon after an apparent skating accident. The man was taken to General Hospital, where he remained unconscious this morning.

A passerby said the victim was skating across the river when she saw him fall through the ice and alerted the police.

Sgt. Jose Velasquez, who responded, pointed out that the ice is still very thin, and said that he had repeatedly warned children and adults of the danger of skating on it at the present time.

_____

_____

Tragedy struck the town of Garland last night when a speeding car went out of control and slammed into a tree, taking the lives of three 16-year-old girls and a 17-year-old boy.

Dead on arrival at Garland Memorial Hospital were Susanne Boulanger, Toni Morris, Renee Delacroix, and Clarence Wilson, the driver of the car.

Police said the car was traveling about 60 miles an hour when the accident occurred. There was no evidence of drugs or alcohol, and neighbors say the victims were all "good kids."

MAN RESCUED FROM RIVER

99 YEARS OLD AND NO COMPLAINTS

FOUR TEENS DIE IN CAR CRASH

THREE ALARM FIRE HITS TRAVEL AGENCY

B. Write other headlines for these same stories. Keep your headlines to no more than two lines of 18 characters (letters and spaces) each.

_____   _____

_____   _____

Skill Objectives: Reading for main idea; writing headlines; learning about newspapers. Discuss why headlines are used. Elicit that they tell the main idea of a story and also help the reader decide whether to read the story. *Part A:* Have a student read the first story aloud, then have the class decide which headline fits it. Do the other stories independently. *Part B:* Elicit that these stories could have different headlines, and encourage students to write new ones for each story.

C. Now write headlines for the following stories.

   Three men wearing ski masks and carrying guns entered the First County Bank this morning and robbed it of several thousand dollars. The robbers entered the bank at 9:02, shortly after it opened for business. They went directly to the three tellers' windows and requested all the money from their cash drawers.

   "They were very polite," said teller Marian Maguire, "but we knew they meant business." There were no customers in the bank, and the robbers were gone within minutes, making their getaway in a green station wagon.

   "Fortunately, no one was hurt," said Carl Jurgens, manager of the bank. Jurgens was drinking coffee in his office when the robbery took place and only heard about it after the robbers had left the bank. He told reporters it would take some time to determine exactly how much money was missing.

   Police are following several leads, but as of late this morning, no arrests had been made.

   A new operation that could save "hundreds of lives" each year was performed at Memorial Hospital this morning. Three surgeons, Doctors Lee Chung, Elly James, and Gopal Mehta, performed the delicate heart procedure on an unnamed patient.

   "We believe this operation is an important breakthrough," a hospital spokesperson told reporters, "but we don't want to say any more about it at this time." Details of the new operation will appear in the *New England Journal of Medicine* later this month.

   Mrs. June May of Irving told this newspaper that she believed the patient was her ex-husband, Justin May. "I know he had a serious heart condition, and I know he checked into Memorial last week," she said. Hospital authorities had no comment. "The patient's right to privacy must be preserved," they said.

D. Clip several stories from your own newspaper. Cut off the headlines, and exchange the stories with classmates. Write headlines for the stories. Then compare them with the headlines that appeared in the newspaper. Do your headlines give a correct idea of the story? Do they call attention to it? Do they present its main idea? Are they as successful in doing these things as those that appeared in the newspaper? Discuss with the class some of the problems in writing headlines.

E. Headlines are not always clear when read out of context. **Look at these headlines. Then write on your paper, or discuss with classmates, what each story was probably about. Use your dictionary for words you don't know.**

1. **CELTS DUMP OPENER AS BUCKS TRIUMPH**

2. **WHITE FLAYS FOES, DEFENDS SCHOOL OUTLAYS**

3. **MT. ST. HELENS THREE YEARS LATER**

4. **BIRD HURTS ELBOW, OUT FOR SEASON**

5. **COMPASS CITES COSTS AS PUBLICATION ENDS**

6. **OLE MAN RIVER REACHES NEW HEIGHTS**

7. **SOX TRADE MARTIN FOR BRAVES' JONES**

8. **MARKET SURGES TO NEW HIGH**

9. **DOW BREAKS RECORD, THIRD DAY IN ROW**

Skill Objectives: Reading for main idea; writing headlines; determining meaning from context. *Part C:* Have a student read the first story aloud, then allow time for each class member to write a headline for it. Have the headlines read and discussed. Assign the second story for independent work. *Parts D and E:* Guide the student discussions. You may wish to put student guesses for Part E on the board and ask students to support their choices. What further information would help them decide?

25

Read All About It

All newspapers use headlines to attract attention. Some writers use sensational headlines to trick people into buying worthless newspapers. The stories that follow these sensational headlines usually turn out to be silly and untrue. **Look at the headlines below. Decide which ones would be likely to appear in a serious newspaper and which are sensational or silly. Label each headline *Serious* or *Silly* on the line under it.** The first one is done for you.

1. **BIGFOOT LIVES, WOMAN CLAIMS**

   Silly

2. **200 KILLED IN PLANE CRASH**

   _____

3. **36 HOMELESS IN APARTMENT FIRE**

   _____

4. **SPACEMEN TOOK ME TO THEIR HOME ON MARS**

   _____

5. **MILLIONAIRE LEAVES FORTUNE TO PET CAT**

   _____

6. **50,000 NEW CARS RECALLED FOR POSSIBLE BRAKE DEFECT**

   _____

7. **THREE GHOSTS LIVE IN MY BASEMENT SAYS 40'S FILM STAR**

   _____

8. **GUILTY VERDICT FOR MAN IN KILLING OF WIFE, 2 KIDS**

   _____

9. **108 DOGS NOT ENOUGH, FAMILY WANTS MORE**

   _____

10. **HURRICANE CAUSES $6 MILLION DAMAGE**

    _____

11. **GIRL CAN READ AT THREE MONTHS**

    _____

12. **THOUSANDS DRIVE TO WORK AS TRAIN WORKERS STRIKE**

    _____

13. **HUSBAND AND WIFE OFFER TO TRADE BABY FOR NEW CAR**

    _____

14. **HIJACKERS TAKE PLANE, HOLD 387 PEOPLE HOSTAGE**

    _____

15. **FAMINE HITS COLONY, THOUSANDS STARVING**

    _____

16. **PSYCHIC PREDICTS QUEEN TO MARRY ROCK SINGER**

    _____

17. **ANGER MOUNTS AS STRIKE AT BRADLEY AUTOMOTIVE ENTERS 12TH WEEK**

    _____

18. **WOMAN LOSES 15 POUNDS IN 2 DAYS WITH WONDER DIET**

    _____

Skill Objectives: Making judgments; categorizing; expanding vocabulary. Read the paragraph at the top of the page orally to the students. Discuss headlines and the kind of tabloid often found in supermarkets. Ask students which newspaper(s) they read. Have they ever read any of the sensational tabloids? Which? Where? When students understand the concept of serious and silly headlines, assign the page for independent work. Review as a group, having students take turns reading headlines and giving their answers; have them explain why they chose one category rather than the other.

Adjective or Adverb?

Adjectives describe or tell about nouns or pronouns. Look at the examples:
Ann's a *pretty* girl. My nightmare was *awful*! That's a *wild* animal.

Adverbs describe or tell about verbs and adjectives. Look at the examples:
She ran *quickly*. It's *extremely* hot. She spoke too *slowly*.

A. **Look at the sentences below. Decide whether the adjective or the adverb completes the sentence best. Circle your answer.** The first one is done for you.

1. He ran (quick / quickly) down the street.

2. My (sad / sadly) friend doesn't like to talk about his problems.

3. Everyone watched the (horrible / horribly) accident in silence.

4. That movie was (amazing / amazingly).

5. I breathed (rapid / rapidly) after I ran up all those steps.

6. Tran is (extreme / extremely) interested in bicycles.

7. Gloria is (awful / awfully) old to be playing with dolls, isn't she?

8. I don't understand algebra very (good / well).

9. That is one of the most (peaceful / peacefully) countries in the world.

10. Those (brave / bravely) soldiers received medals for their actions.

11. The ocean waves slapped (loud / loudly) against the rocks.

12. Yoshiko tiptoed out of the baby's room (quiet / quietly).

13. That house is too (expensive / expensively) for us.

14. I thought those paintings were (incredible / incredibly) ugly.

15. Everyone is (hungry / hungrily) for supper.

16. The students behaved (bad / badly) when their teacher was away.

17. She spoke (insolent / insolently) to her parents.

18. The children waited (hungry / hungrily) for their lunch.

19. I listened (patient / patiently) to the policeman's warning.

20. I can't go; I'm (terrible / terribly) sick.

B. **Now write a sentence on your paper for each of the following words. Make sure you use the adjectives as adjectives and the adverbs as adverbs.**

serious	strange	nervous	beautiful	recent
seriously	strangley	nervously	beautifully	recently

Skill Objectives: Choosing between adjectives and adverbs; building vocabulary; internalizing grammar rules. Review the boxed explanation of adjectives and adverbs at the top of the page. Make sure that students understand the concept of nouns, pronouns, and verbs as well as adjectives and adverbs. Do a few examples as a class, then assign students independent time to complete the page on their own. Review the page together, with students reading the complete sentences aloud. Have students explain their choices.

27

Dear Dot

Dear Dot—

How can I make friends? I am new in town, and I don't have any friends here yet. Before I came here, I had lots of friends, but they were the people I grew up with. They were always my friends. I don't remember getting to know them, they were just always there from the first grade. I have been here for six weeks now, and some of the kids are starting to smile and say hello, but I don't really have any friends yet. What can I do?

Lonely

Discuss each of the questions in class. Then write your answers.

1. Do most people have this problem when they move? Why or why not? _____
_____
_____

2. What are some good places to make new friends? _____
_____
_____

3. How should a person act when he or she is trying to make new friends? _____
_____
_____

4. How long does it usually take to make new friends? _____
_____

5. Are the first people you meet always likely to become good friends? Why or why not?
_____
_____

Write About It

Now put yourself in Dot's place. Write a helpful answer to Lonely. Remember, you want to help solve the problem, not make fun of the writer or criticize.

Dear Lonely—

_____
_____
_____
_____
_____
_____
_____
_____

Skill Objectives: Reading for main idea; making inferences; generalizing from experience; expressing opinions in writing. Have students read the letter. Discuss each question in class. Encourage free expression of opinion, but be sure students can support their opinions. Then have students write answers to the questions. Suggest that they use these answers as the basis for their letters. You may wish to assign the letter-writing activity as homework.

Which One Is It?

In English, one statement often *implies* or *includes* another idea. Look at the example below. Read the sentence in boldface type. Then look at the three sentences under it. Which one is implied by the **boldfaced** sentence? In other words, which one *has to* be true if the **boldfaced** sentence is true?

Example: **Karl has been an engineer for five years.**

    a. He's an engineer now.
    b. He was an engineer, but he isn't one now.
    c. He is going to be an engineer.

You should have chosen *a*. The structure "has been . . . for" implies an action or a condition that started in the past and is still going on. If Karl has been an engineer for five years, he is still an engineer, so *a* is correct.

A. Now look at each of the items below. Choose the answer that is implied by the bold-faced statement and circle it.

1. **Kathy has already taken a shower.**
   a. She is going to take a shower.
   b. She took a shower.
   c. She takes a shower every morning.

2. **Paul has worked at the bank for ten years.**
   a. He is going to work at the bank.
   b. He works at the bank.
   c. He doesn't work at the bank anymore.

3. **Carla and Roberto have been students for seven years.**
   a. They plan to study in the future.
   b. They studied seven years ago and stopped studying.
   c. They are students.

4. **I have seen the movie *Big* six times.**
   a. I saw the movie.
   b. I'm going to see the movie.
   c. I want to see the movie.

5. **You have lived in the United States for three years.**
   a. You came to the United States three years ago.
   b. You plan to live in the United States three years from now.
   c. You have come to the United States three times.

6. **Tom has been in the hospital for a week.**
   a. He was in the hospital, but he isn't there now.
   b. He is going to go to the hospital.
   c. He's in the hospital now.

B. Circle the correct answers to the questions.

1. **When you saw John, what was he doing?**
   a. He played soccer.
   b. He was playing soccer.
   c. He plays soccer.

2. **Has Lisa ever broken her leg?**
   a. Yes, she did.
   b. Yes, she was.
   c. Yes, she has.

Skill Objectives: Using present perfect tense; using time expressions with *for*; understanding implied meaning. Teach/review the present perfect tense. Discuss implied meanings. Be sure students understand that a meaning can be implied without being specifically stated. Do the example; have a volunteer explain why *a* is correct. *Part A:* Do several items orally, discussing each one, then assign as written work. *Part B:* Do the first item orally, discuss why *b* is correct, then assign the second item as written work.

Luisa and Nga

Rewrite the following paragraphs, using the correct form of the verb in parentheses. Use only the simple past (ate) or the present perfect (has eaten).

Luisa and Nga (COME) to the United States three years ago. When they first (START) school, they (BE) very nervous, because they (NOT-SPEAK) any English. Now they speak English very well, of course, because they (LIVE) here for three years and (STUDY) the language.

After school, Luisa works at a small supermarket near her house. She (WORK) at the store for six months. Last month she (WORK) there two afternoons a week, but now she works three afternoons a week.

Nga doesn't work after school because when she finishes her homework, she teaches English to her aunt and uncle who (ARRIVE) from Vietnam a month ago. In the past month, her aunt and uncle (LEARN) 200 new words, and Nga (ALREADY-TEACH) them the past tense. When Nga first (BEGIN) teaching them, she (NOT-HAVE) much patience, but now she feels more comfortable. As a matter of fact, she (ALREADY-DECIDE) that when she graduates from high school, she wants to go to college and study education!

Luisa's father is from Puerto Rico and her mother is from the Dominican Republic. Her parents first (MEET) in Miami, when they (BE) on vacation. Several years later, they (GET) married. They (LIVE) in Mexico for many years before they (MOVE) to Texas three years ago.

_____

_____

_____

_____

_____

_____

_____

_____

_____

_____

_____

_____

_____

_____

_____

_____

_____

_____

_____

_____

Skill Objectives: Choosing between simple past and present perfect; using context to determine correct tense. Read the instructions with the class. Emphasize that they must use only the simple past or past perfect tense of the verb in parentheses. Do the first paragraph orally, and discuss why the first four verbs should be simple past and the last two, past perfect. Then assign the page, perhaps as homework. Be sure students understand they are to rewrite the entire story. They may use more paper if necessary.

The Past Perfect

Read these rules about forming and using the past perfect tense.

The past perfect tense is formed with *had* and the past participle.

I had seen	We had seen
You had seen	You had seen
He had seen	
She had seen	They had seen
It had seen	

The past perfect tense describes an action that took place in the past before another past action.

Example: Yesterday

```
        8:00              9:00
         |-----------------|
     I wrote           I mailed
     a letter          the letter
```

I *mailed* the letter after I *had written* it.

A. Use the past perfect in the following sentences. The first one is done for you.

1. When I arrived at the bus station, the bus _____ *had left* _____ (leave).

2. The bank _____ (close) five minutes before I got there.

3. When we got to the theater, the movie _____ (start).

4. Mrs. Jones called the doctor because her son _____ (eat) twenty aspirin.

5. Before I took the test, I _____ (study) for it.

B. Combine the following sentences into one sentence. Use the past tense and the past perfect.

Example: a. First, I did my homework.
b. Then, I watched television.

After I had done my homework, I watched television.
(or) I watched television after I had done my homework.

1. First I washed the dishes.
   Then I dried them.
   1. _____

2. First I took a bath.
   Then I got dressed.
   2. _____

3. First I cooked dinner.
   Then I ate it.
   3. _____

4. First I took out a loan.
   Then I bought the car.
   4. _____

5. First I got on the bus.
   Then I paid my fare.
   5. _____

Skill Objectives: Forming and using the past perfect; combining sentences using *after*. Teach/review the formation of the past perfect tense. Do the example; be sure students understand the relation between the two past actions. Ask for other examples and put them on the board. *Part A:* Discuss the first item, then assign as written work. *Part B:* Point out the two ways of combining the sentences; tell students they may use either. Do the first item orally, then assign as written work.

The Break-In

Before   After

Last night somebody entered the principal's office. **What did the robber do?** The first answer is done for you.

1. *The robber stole the electric typewriter.*

2. _____

3. _____

4. _____

5. _____

6. _____

7. _____

8. _____

When the principal arrived at seven o'clock the next morning, she saw what the robber had done. She called the police and filed a report. **What did the principal say to the police?** The first answer is done for you.

1. *She said that someone had stolen the electric typewriter.*

2. _____

3. _____

4. _____

5. _____

6. _____

7. _____

8. _____

Skill Objectives: Using the simple past and past perfect; understanding and using reported speech. Elicit that the pictures show a principal's office before and after a break-in. Tell the students to use the pictures to answer "What did the robber do?" Discuss several answers; elicit why the simple past tense is used. Point out that the second part of the page asks "What did the principal say?" Discuss why the past perfect tense is used for reported speech. Do several items orally, then assign as written work.

32

What the Puzzler Has Done

Write the words in the right places. Number 1 Across and number 1 Down are done for you.

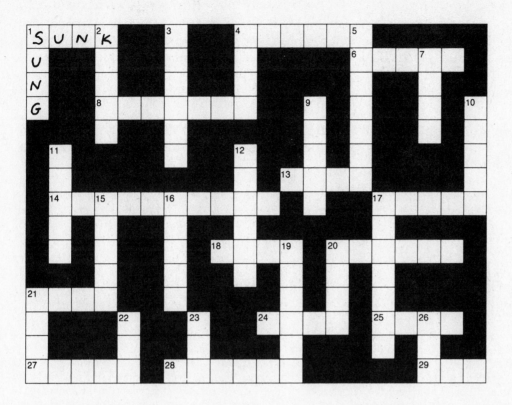

Across

1. What the ship has done.
4. What the professor has done.
6. What the listener has done.
8. What the novelist has done.
13. What the sad man has done.
14. What the successful student has done.
17. What the girl who has read page 1 has done.
18. What the finders have done.
20. What the lecturer has done.
21. What the eyes have done.
24. What the story teller has done.
25. What the hands have done.
27. What the words have done.
28. What the thief has done.
29. What the miners have done.

Down

1. What the soprano has done.
2. What the successful test taker has done.
3. What the receivers of gifts have done.
4. What the paper shredder has done.
5. What the philosophers have done.
7. What the bells have done.
9. What the diners have done.
10. What the pilot has done.
11. What the thirsty children have done.
12. What the careless waiters have done.
15. What the artists have done.
16. What the dreamers have done.
17. What the mail carrier has done.
19. What the baseball player has done.
20. What the speaker has done.
21. What the swimmers have done.
22. What the new neighbors have done.
23. What the people in chairs have done.
26. What the team's captain has done.

(Answers on page 125)

Skill Objectives: Reviewing the present perfect; using past participles. Do the first few across and down clues with the class. Be sure students understand how to fill in a crossword puzzle; elicit the way in which the across and down answers interlock. Tell students they may check spelling with a dictionary. You may wish to assign the puzzle as homework or have students work on it in pairs.

33

Reading the Newspaper: The News Story

A news story, or article, is a report of something that happened. A good news story tells what happened, who it happened to, when it happened, where it happened, and sometimes why it happened.

Because people are busy, and because there are many stories in each issue of a newspaper, reporters try to put the "what, who, when, where, and why" into the first, or "lead" paragraph. This gives busy readers the basic facts. If they want to find out more about the happening, they can read the rest of the story.

A. Read the two stories below. Both tell about the same event. Which one includes the important w's in its lead paragraph? After you have read the stories, answer the questions about them.

STORY A

MOTHER KIDNAPS OWN CHILD

by Thomas Carnes

A desperate father today accused his ex-wife of kidnapping their daughter from her front yard last night. Amos Orson, of 30 Banks Road, said Melinda, 7, was missing from the yard soon after a red car had stopped there. He said he was sure that Mrs. Marla Orson, angered at a court decision that gave Amos Orson custody, had taken the law into her own hands and snatched her daughter.

Orson said that Melinda had been playing in the yard just before the car drove up. When he looked out later, both the car and Melinda were gone.

The Orsons were divorced last year. A long custody battle, in which each accused the other of being an unfit parent, ended with the award of Melinda, their only child, to her father. Orson told Inspector Josephine Riley that Marla had refused to accept the decision. He also said he had heard she had recently bought a red car.

Police were without comment on Orson's accusations. "It's one of the leads we'll be looking into," Riley told reporters, "but only one."

Parental kidnapping is not uncommon, Professor John Prout of Maslow College's Family Crisis Center told this reporter. "Child custody is the festering thorn in most divorces," he said, and the losers often refuse to abide by court decisions.

STORY B

FATHER ACCUSES EX-WIFE OF KIDNAPPING CHILD, 7

by Thomas Carnes

An accusation of parental kidnapping was made today as a desperate father reported the apparent abduction of his seven-year-old daughter to police. The local resident said he "knew" that his ex-wife had taken the child. The couple was divorced last year, and custody of the daughter, their only child, was awarded to the father.

The man, identified as Amos Orson of 30 Banks Road, said he had been awarded custody of Melinda, 7, when the couple was divorced. He said Melinda was playing in the yard of his house when he saw a red car drive up. Later, when he looked out, Melinda was gone.

Orson said his ex-wife, Marla, was a "sorehead" and had never agreed with the court's decision to give custody to him. "And I heard she just got a new red car," he told Riley.

Parental kidnapping is not uncommon, Professor John Prout of Maslow College's Family Crisis Center told this reporter. "Child custody is the festering thorn in most divorces," he said, and parents often try to take matters into their own hands.

Police were without comment on Orson's accusations. "It's one of the leads we'll be looking into," Riley told reporters, "but only one."

Skill Objectives: Organizing information; understanding news stories; identifying reported speech and direct quotations. Discuss the characteristics of a news story and the reasons for putting the basic facts into the first or "lead" paragraph. Have volunteers read the two stories aloud, and have the class compare and discuss them. Call attention to the use of reported speech, and elicit that the past perfect tense is used. Point out that both stories also use direct quotations, identified by quotation marks.

34

1. Which story includes the five w's in the first paragraph? Circle your answer.

   Story A   Story B

2. What is the main idea of the stories? Circle your answer.
   a. A little girl disappeared from her yard after a red car drove up.
   b. Parents often kidnap their children if they have not been granted custody.
   c. A father was awarded custody of his seven-year-old daughter.
   d. A father accused his ex-wife of kidnapping their seven-year-old daughter.

3. What was Melinda doing before she disappeared? _____
   _____

4. What two reasons did Mr. Orson give for believing his ex-wife had taken Melinda? _____
   _____
   _____

5. The stories include a "byline." Where does it come in the story? What does it tell? Why is it called a byline? (You may need to use your dictionary.)
   _____
   _____
   _____

6. Which headline is the better one? Give two reasons why. _____
   _____
   _____
   _____

B. News stories or articles are written in an "inverted pyramid" form. As you have seen, this means that the most important facts in the story come in the first paragraph, less important facts in the later paragraphs. This form makes it possible for a reader to find out quickly what the story is about. It also makes it possible for an editor to cut the story easily to make it fit the available space. The editor can do this simply by removing paragraphs from the end of the story.

On your paper, write a news story of your own. Use the following facts:
- The mayor called a press conference.
- The conference was at 11:00 AM yesterday.
- The conference was to announce that Micro-Byte, a large computer company, will build an office and factory in the city.
- The president of the computer company spoke at the meeting. He said, "I am enthusiastic about coming here." He called the city forward-looking and progressive. He said he looked forward to working with the residents of the city.
- Building will start next month, with completion planned for a year from now.
- The company expects to employ about 2500 workers in the new facility.

Add other facts if you wish to. Do not put in your own opinion, however. A news story is a report of what happened, not a place to comment on it. It is all right to report other peoples' opinions—they are news. But the reporter's opinions are best omitted from a news story. (Other kinds of articles—columns, editorials, "feature" stories—can include the writer's opinions, however.)

Skill Objectives: Reading for main idea and details; organizing information; making judgments; writing news stories. *Part A:* Do the questions orally with the class, then assign as written work. *Part B:* Discuss the concept of the "inverted pyramid." Elicit that the news-story structure can be helpful in writing any kind of report. Call attention to the need for objectivity in news stories, and discuss the other kinds of writing found in newspapers in which opinion is acceptable or desirable.

35

Preparing for Tests: Inferences and Conclusions

One of the oldest legends in Europe is the story of King Arthur and his Knights of the Round Table. According to the legend, the Knights of the Round Table did many heroic things. They killed dragons and rescued damsels in distress. But they are best known because of their quest or search for the Holy Grail.

The Holy Grail was the chalice or cup that Jesus drank from at the Last Supper. The legend says that a disciple named Joseph of Arimathea used the cup to catch blood from Jesus' wounds. Joseph later took the Grail to England. It disappeared centuries later when one of Joseph's descendents was wounded. King Arthur's knights set out to find it.

The legend said that only a person who was pure in heart could find the grail. Three knights, Sir Bors, Sir Percival, and Sir Galahad finally found it.

The legend of King Arthur and his knights has been told for 1400 years. Nobody today knows if there really was a King Arthur or a search for the Holy Grail. Some historians think that Arthur was a real person and that he was so powerful that people made up the legend around him. What do you think?

Circle the best answer for each question. The first one is done for you.

1. A "damsel in distress" is

   a. a horse in anguish.

   b. a kingdom in peril.

   c. a woman in danger.

   d. a knight in trouble.

2. It may be inferred from the selection that the Holy Grail was valuable because

   a. it was made of pure gold.

   b. it belonged to King Arthur.

   c. it came from a far-away place.

   d. it once held the blood of Jesus.

3. It can be concluded that Sir Bors, Sir Percival, and Sir Galahad were

   a. very lucky

   b. pure in heart

   c. sons of King Arthur

   d. descendents of Joseph of Arimathea

4. Which of the following words does not belong with the others?

   a. chalice   b. Grail   c. cup   d. quest

5. The author indicates that

   a. King Arthur found the Holy Grail.

   b. No one knows for certain what is true about the Holy Grail.

   c. The Knights of the Round Table were cruel and greedy.

   d. Joseph of Arimathea was a British citizen.

BRITISH KNIGHTS

Skill Objectives: Reading for inference; finding specific information; drawing conclusions. Explain to students that this exercise is typical of reading items on standardized tests. Explain the importance of reading carefully but quickly. You may want to time the students, so that they get used to pacing themselves on a reading passage and its associated questions. (Six minutes is the suggested time limit for this on some standardized tests.) After students have completed the page, reread the passage orally, and have students tell you their answers to the questions. Discuss/explain all answers, paying special attention to inference questions.

Dear Dot

Dear Dot—

I'm fifteen years old. I do very well in school, and I work part time three days a week. After I finish my homework, I like to watch television, but my parents insist that I need my rest, and I have to be in bed by 10:00. I think I'm old enough to decide my own bedtime and choose my own television shows. I think I have shown my parents that I am responsible by getting good grades and holding a job. How else can I convince them to let me make my own decisions in this matter?

Paulette

Discuss each of the questions in class. Then write your answers.

1. Do parents have the right to control television watching and bedtime hours?
   Why or why not? _____

   _____

2. When do children become responsible for themselves? Give reasons for your answer.

   _____

   _____

3. Is Paulette responsible? Why or why not? _____

   _____

4. How can Paulette change her parents' minds? _____

   _____

Write About It

Now put yourself in Dot's place. Write a helpful answer to Paulette. Remember, you want to help her solve her problem, not make fun of her or criticize her.

Dear Paulette—

_____

_____

_____

_____

_____

_____

_____

_____

_____

Skill Objectives: Reading for main idea; making inferences; making judgments; expressing opinions in writing. Have students read the letter. Discuss each question in class. Encourage free expression of opinion, but be sure students can support their opinions. Then have students write answers to the questions. Suggest that they use these answers as the basis for their letters. You may wish to assign the letter-writing activity as homework.

37

Tag Endings

A "tag ending" is a short question that follows a statement. It asks the listener to agree or disagree with the statement, to confirm it or deny it. A tag ending (or "tag question") can be answered with a simple "yes" or "no," or it can be answered with a longer statement. To find the verb to use in the tag ending, in your mind change a positive statement to a negative question. "You opened the window" becomes "Didn't you open the window?" The statement with its tag ending then is "You opened the window *didn't you*?" Look at the examples:

The traffic is heavy today, _____*isn't it*_____ ?

You watched the football game on TV _____*didn't you*_____ ?

A. Add tag endings to these statements. Look at the tense of the verb and then decide what the tag ending should be.

1. Lisa can drive a car, _____?

2. You'll be back before noon, _____?

3. Jim is coming to my party, _____?

4. I should read the direction before taking the medicine, _____?

5. You were absent from school yesterday, _____?

6. We had a lot of homework last night, _____?

7. Susan will graduate in June, _____?

8. She's already done her homework, _____?

9. It was hot yesterday, _____?

10. The bus comes at 10:15, _____?

11. It takes five hours to fly to New York, _____?

12. He has been working at the bank for a long time, _____?

B. Now add tag endings to these statements, then ask the questions to two students in your class. Ask the students to answer yes or no. Record your answers.

	Student 1	Student 2
1. You're from China, _____?		
2. You live in Boston, _____?		
3. You have a driver's license, _____?		
4. You did your English homework, _____?		
5. You were 15 last year, _____?		
6. You will graduate next year, _____?		
7. You play volleyball, _____?		
8. You saw the movie *E.T.*, _____?		
9. You've been in the U.S. for a year, _____?		
10. You can swim, _____?		

Skill Objectives: Forming and using tag endings; asking and answering questions; plotting information on charts. Read the introductory paragraph with the class. Be sure students understand how to form tag endings. *Part A:* Do the items orally, then assign as written work. *Part B:* Have volunteers give tag endings for the first three items. Then have students complete the tag endings independently and ask and record answers to the questions. Later, have students report their results to the class.

What Do You Know?

Test yourself. Make the following statements into questions by adding tag endings. Then answer the questions. Use an encyclopedia or atlas if you need to.

A. Use a negative tag ending with a positive statement. The first two are done for you. Use them as models.

1. The capital of California is San Francisco, _____isn't it_____?
   No, it's Sacramento.

2. New Hampshire has a short coastline, _____doesn't it_____?
   Yes, it does.

3. Alaska is the largest state, _____?
   _____

4. People from Sweden are Swiss, _____?
   _____

5. The Dominican Republic and Haiti share the same island, _____?
   _____

6. Much of the world's gold comes from South Africa, _____?
   _____

7. The official languages of Canada are English and Spanish, _____?
   _____

B. Use an affirmative tag ending with a negative statement. The first two are done for you. Use them as models.

1. Lima isn't the capital of Peru, _____is it_____?
   Yes, it is!

2. Kangaroos don't live in Austria, _____do they_____?
   No, they live in Australia.

3. Australia isn't a continent, _____?
   _____

4. Saudi Arabia doesn't export oil, _____?
   _____

5. People in Switzerland don't speak Dutch, _____?
   _____

6. Brazilians aren't very fond of coffee, _____?
   _____

7. The Pacific isn't the largest ocean, _____?
   _____

Skill Objectives: Forming and using tag endings; using reference materials; building knowledge of world geography. Review the formation of tag endings; remind students that positive statements take negative tag questions, and point out that negative statements take positive tag questions. Stress that students are not expected to know the answers to many of the items on the page but are to use an encyclopedia or atlas. Do the examples for each part with the class before assigning that part as written work.

Voting: Your Part in Government

One of the basic principles of the United States government is *popular sovereignty.* Popular means "of the people." Sovereignty means "rule" or "power." So the government is based on the idea that the people are the rulers. They hold all the power.

The people exercise (use) this power in several different ways, but the most important one is voting. The people vote for the President and Vice President every four years. They vote for senators and members of the House of Representatives every two years. They also vote for members of their state legislature (the group that makes state laws), their state governor, and for many other officials in their state, county, and city or town.

To vote, a person has to be a citizen, and has to be at least 18 years old. Before voting, he or she has to register. (In North Dakota and in parts of some other states, this is not necessary.) The person has to prove that he or she is a citizen of the United States and a resident of the state in which he or she will vote.

Voting is done in several ways. In some areas, the voter is given a *ballot,* a piece of paper with the names of the different candidates for each office printed on it. The voter marks an X next to the names of the candidates he or she prefers.

In other areas, voting is done by machine. The voter moves a lever down under the names of the candidates he or she is voting for. After all choices are made, the voter pulls another lever to record the vote and prepare the machine for the next voter.

Some areas use a punch card method. The voter punches holes next to the names of the chosen candidates. After everyone has voted, the cards are put into a computer that counts the number of holes punched for each candidate.

PRESIDENT vote for one			
G. Washington	1 ▶	1	
T. Jefferson	2 ▶	2	
J. Q. Adams	3 ▶	3	
		4	
VICE PRESIDENT vote for one		5	
		6	
D. Eisenhower	7 ▶	7	
A. Lincoln	8 ▶	8	
T. Roosevelt	9 ▶	9	
H. Truman	10 ▶	10	

PUNCH CARD METHOD

In all these methods, the voter's choice is *secret.* No one but the voter knows how he or she voted.

Almost all citizens over the age of 18 have the right to vote. Some states do not let people vote who have been convicted of certain crimes. No state allows people in mental hospitals to vote.

Although nearly all citizens over 18 can vote today, this was not always true. When the Constitution was adopted, no state allowed women to vote. In many states a man had to own property or belong to a particular church. Slaves could not vote. No one under 21 could vote. Gradually these limits on voting rights were eliminated. Blacks gained the right to vote in 1870, but some states set up tests or passed taxes that made it difficult or impossible for many of them to vote. Some states allowed women to vote starting in 1869 but not until 1920 could all American women vote. Bars to black voting were removed in the 1960s and 1970s, and the voting age was reduced to 18 in 1971.

Skill Objectives: Reading for details; making judgments; learning about U.S. government. Discuss voting with the class. Have any of them voted? Have their parents or friends? Ask why voting is important. Then read the essay to the class or have it read by one or more students. Allow time for silent rereading.

A. **Refer to the article on voting on the previous page. Read the statements below. If the statement is true, write *T*. If the statement is false, write *F*. If the story doesn't give you enough information to know if the statement is true or false, write *?*.** The first two are done for you.

___*T*___ 1. Popular sovereignty means that the people hold the power.

___*?*___ 2. Voters always vote in every election.

_____ 3. Americans elect a new president every four years.

_____ 4. Americans elect members of the Senate and House of Representatives every four years.

_____ 5. Americans elect governors every four years.

_____ 6. You must be 18 and a citizen to be able to vote.

_____ 7. You must also be a resident of the state for one year.

_____ 8. There are two different ways to vote: by paper ballot and punch card.

_____ 9. Most people vote by computer.

_____ 10. The voter's choice is always secret.

_____ 11. People usually vote in schools or government buildings.

_____ 12. Many Black Americans couldn't vote before 1960.

_____ 13. People in mental hospitals can vote.

_____ 14. Women couldn't vote before 1960.

_____ 15. Before 1971 the legal voting age was 21.

B. You read in the article that the voting age was reduced to 18 in 1971. Before that year it was 21 in most states. Are 18-year-olds mature enough to vote? Why or why not? **Decide how you feel about the issue and then write an essay supporting your decision. Use more paper if you need to.**

_____

_____

_____

_____

_____

_____

_____

_____

_____

_____

_____

Skill Objectives: Reading for details; supporting opinions in writing. *Part A:* Review the True, False, question mark format. Emphasize that if the article does not provide information for the answer, the question mark must be used, even if the student knows from other sources that the sentence is true or false. *Part B:* Read the instructions orally and discuss the question with the class. You may wish to have students write their essays as homework.

41

And So Do I

Two sentences describing the same action can be combined into one sentence in several ways. Look at the examples below:

Bonnie missed the bus. Fred missed the bus.

a. Bonnie missed the bus, and Fred did, too.
b. Bonnie missed the bus, and so did Fred.

Notice that the verb in the tag phrase of the combined sentence ("... Fred *did,* too.") matches the verb form used in the two sentences.

Here's another example.

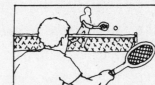

I like to play tennis. Ronald likes to play tennis.

a. I like to play tennis, and Ronald does, too.
b. I like to play tennis, and so does Ronald.

Combine each of the following sentences in two ways.

1. Carla went to the movies last night. I went to the movies last night.

    a. _____

    b. _____

2. Janet can drive a car. Tom can drive a car.

    a. _____

    b. _____

3. George will graduate in June. I will graduate in June.

    a. _____

    b. _____

4. I could name all the Presidents. Susan could name all the Presidents.

    a. _____

    b. _____

5. My father is watching TV now. My sisters are watching TV now.

    a. _____

    b. _____

6. You have a bad cold. I have a bad cold.

    a. _____

    b. _____

7. Linda Ronstadt is a singer. Diana Ross is a singer.

    a. _____

    b. _____

8. Fish live in the ocean. Whales live in the ocean.

    a. _____

    b. _____

Skill Objectives: Combining sentences using *too* and *so*; choosing correct tenses; writing alternate forms of a sentence. Go over the examples with the class. Be sure students understand why *did* is used in the first example and *does* in the second. Do all items orally with the class, then assign as written work. Extension: Discuss other ways in which the sentences could be combined (*Ronald and I . . ., Both Ronald and I . . .*), and have students write additional answers for each item.

Either, Neither

Either and *neither* can be used to combine two negative statements into one. Look at the example. Notice that there are two ways of combining the sentences. One uses *either* and the other uses *neither.*

Example: Susan doesn't like to play tennis. I don't like to play tennis.

a. Susan doesn't like to play tennis, and I don't either.
b. Susan doesn't like to play tennis, and neither do I.

Now combine the pairs of sentences below. Do each pair both ways.

1. I don't have any money. George doesn't have any money.

    a. _____

    b. _____

2. Mr. Ross didn't go to work yesterday. I didn't go to work yesterday.

    a. _____

    b. _____

3. David can't speak Russian. Rosita can't speak Russian.

    a. _____

    b. _____

4. Carlos isn't from Lebanon. John isn't from Lebanon.

    a. _____

    b. _____

5. Paul wasn't in class yesterday. Carla and Ana weren't in class yesterday.

    a. _____

    b. _____

6. I won't graduate until next year. Linda and Jerry won't graduate until next year.

    a. _____

    b. _____

7. Kenneth isn't feeling well today. I am not feeling well today.

    a. _____

    b. _____

8. Mr. and Mrs. Garcia aren't going to buy a new car. You are not going to buy a new car.

    a. _____

    b. _____

9. Fred doesn't like Chinese food. I don't like Chinese food.

    a. _____

    b. _____

Skill Objectives: Combining sentences with *either* and *neither*; writing alternate forms of a sentence. Review the use of *so* and *too* to combine positive sentences (page 42). Point out that negative sentences are combined another way, using *either* or *neither*. (Tell students that these can be pronounced with either a long *i* or long *e* sound; the long *e* is more common in the United States.) Go over the examples, then do all items orally before assigning as written work.

Reading the Newspaper: The Feature Story

Use a description and illustrations to understand a feature story; then write one.

Newspapers usually include more than just news stories. They also include feature stories. A feature is not usually about something that has just taken place. Instead it takes a look at things the readers are talking or thinking about. Some features are humorous, designed to give pleasure and entertain the reader. Others provide background information about subjects in which readers are likely to be interested. Many newspapers use different kinds of features on different days. They will have stories about books and the arts one day each week, and stories about business developments another day. They will have stories about education another day, and stories about science on still another day. Read the story below and decide the category it belongs in. Then answer the questions that follow it.

OUR LAKES: ARE THEY IN TROUBLE?

People like lakes to be clean, sparkling, and clear. And many lakes fit this description. To a scientist, these lakes are "oligotrophic," a word made from two Greek roots meaning "few" and "nutrients." Because these lakes have few nutrients—things that feed plants—they are clear. There are few algae (microscopic plants) in oligotrophic lakes, and lots of oxygen. The water in these lakes is cold and deep. Sunlight travels nearly to the bottom, adding to the lakes' clearness.

Not all lakes are oligotrophic. There is another kind of lake with water that is green, often covered with scum, and warm. Scientists call these lakes "eutrophic," meaning "well nourished." The water in these lakes is full of nutrients which feed algae and other plants. These plants decay and fall to the bottom, building a deep layer of organic sediment. Sunlight cannot travel to the deep waters because of the plant life.

Oligotrophic lakes are relatively young. Eutrophic lakes are older. As lakes age, they become increasingly eutrophic.

How Lakes Change

All oligotrophic lakes will someday become eutrophic as they fill with nutrients and chemicals. It is natural for nutrients from the soil around a lake to wash into it. Heavy rains may carry soil into the lake. Or they may dissolve the nutrients out of the soil and carry them into the lake in liquid form.

When enough nutrients and chemicals gather in a lake, the lake changes from oligotrophic to eutrophic. The nutrients allow more and more plants to grow in the lake. The dead plants decay. The decay, or rotting process, takes oxygen from the water. The green water absorbs sunlight and warms up. Cold-water fish, such as salmon and trout, die out, and warm-water fish, such as bass, replace them.

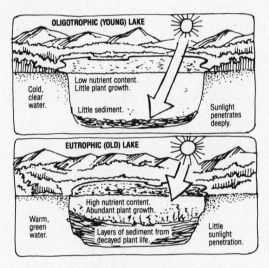

OLIGOTROPHIC (YOUNG) LAKE

Cold, clear water.

Low nutrient content. Little plant growth.

Little sediment.

Sunlight penetrates deeply.

EUTROPHIC (OLD) LAKE

Warm, green water.

High nutrient content. Abundant plant growth.

Layers of sediment from decayed plant life.

Little sunlight penetration.

What Can We Do?

Natural eutrophication, the change from an oligotrophic lake to a eutrophic one, normally takes thousands of years. Today, however, it is happening much more rapidly. What has happened to speed up the process?

What has happened is peoples' activities. A lake near a farm, for example, gets many more nutrients than a lake near a forest. This is because the farmer puts fertilizer on the fields, and much of this fertilizer eventually washes down into the lake. Homes and factories also produce nutrients and chemicals that reach lakes near them. These and other activities of people can turn a lake green and warm in ten years.

Yes, our lakes are in trouble. We need to learn how to care for them. We may not be able to stop the eutrophication process competely, but we can control what goes into our lakes. We can give them the TLC—tender loving care—that will keep them the way we want them, clean, clear, and sparkling.

Skill Objectives: Reading for details; understanding different types of informative writing; learning scientific/technical vocabulary; understanding scientific illustrations. Read the paragraph at the top of the page and discuss the difference between feature stories and news stories. Have students volunteer examples that point out the difference. Ask why many newspapers print a weekly science section; elicit the importance of science and technology in today's world. Preview some of the scientific vocabulary in the article and call attention to the way in which it is explained to the reader. Help students see how the illustrations reinforce the ideas in the story. Allow time for students to read the story.

A. Read the article on page 44 and use it to answer these questions. Use complete sentences. Use more paper if you need to.

1. What is an oligotrophic lake? _____
_____
_____

2. What is a eutrophic lake? _____
_____
_____

3. How do oligotrophic lakes become eutrophic lakes? _____
_____
_____
_____

4. How do nutrients get into a lake naturally.? _____
_____
_____

5. What do plants do in a eutrophic lake? _____
_____
_____

6. What kind of lake do salmon and trout prefer? _____
_____

7. How long does it normally take a lake to change from oligotrophic to eutrophic?
_____

8. What happens when peoples' activities add too many nutrients to a lake? _____
_____

B. *Olig-* and *eu-* are prefixes used in a number of words. **Look up the following words in a dictionary and write a sentence using each one. Try to write your sentence so that the reader will understand the meaning of the word from context.**

1. oligarchy _____

2. oligopoly _____

3. euphonious _____

4. eupeptic _____

C. Find out about an environmental problem in your area. Write a feature story that explains the problem. In your story, make sure to include the causes of the problem, the effects of the problem, and possible solutions to the problem.

Skill Objectives: Reading for specific information; understanding cause and effect; writing a scientific/technical feature story. Discuss the story on page 44. *Part A:* Work through the eight questions orally as a class before assigning them as independent written work. *Part B:* Have students read their sentences aloud and explain them to the class. *Part C:* Talk about environmental issues in your area. Have students individually or in small groups pick an environmental issue that interests them and write a feature story about it. Refer them to local newspapers and magazines for specific information; your school librarian may be able to help. An encyclopedia can be used to check technical facts—if it's up to date!

Preparing for Tests:
Stated and Implied Ideas (1)

The Great Barrier Reef lies off the east coast of Australia. It is 1200 miles long and forms a boundary, or sea barrier, between Australia and New Zealand. The reef is made of coral, a kind of stone formed from the skeletons of millions of small sea animals. As living coral animals die, their skeletons are added to the reef.

The Great Barrier Reef is important to Australia as a source of tourist trade. Unfortunately, tourists have brought trouble to the reef. Since the 1960s, Crown of Thorns starfish have been eating the living coral animals. Large segments of the reef have worn away because new coral-forming skeletons have not been added to them. This has happened because tourists have killed the natural enemy of the starfish, the sea triton, in great numbers in order to collect the tritons' beautiful shells. As more and more tritons are killed, fewer are left to attack the starfish and keep them from eating the coral animals. If the Great Barrier Reef is to continue to exist, sea tritons must be re-introduced into the waters around it.

SEA TRITON

CROWN OF THORNS STARFISH

Circle the best answer for each question.

1. The Great Barrier Reef is
   a. between Austria and New Zealand
   b. dangerous to tourists
   c. composed of skeletons
   d. over 1200 miles deep in the ocean

2. The Great Barrier Reef provides all of the following except
   a. beautiful shells
   b. capital from tourist dollars
   c. a natural boundary between two countries
   d. a home for sharks and other large fish

3. There are more starfish than usual in the waters around the reef now because
   a. the starfish love to eat coral
   b. tourists want to see the starfish more than the coral
   c. the natural enemy of the starfish has been almost killed off
   d. tritons have stopped eating starfish and started eating other food

4. To solve the problem of the Great Barrier Reef, environmentalists must
   a. kill more starfish
   b. relocate the barrier reef
   c. build up the triton population
   d. stop all tourist trade along the reef

5. The author would most likely agree that
   a. tourists should be allowed to take as many shells as they want
   b. people should not visit the Great Barrier Reef
   c. the Great Barrier Reef must be protected or it will be lost
   d. starfish must be killed in large numbers to preserve the reef

Skill Objectives: Reading for inference; finding specific information; understanding stated and implied ideas. This page, like page 36, is in a format typical of reading exercises in standardized tests. Reemphasize the importance of reading carefully but quickly. You may want to time the students so that they get used to pacing themselves on a reading passage and the associated questions. Six minutes is suggested as a time limit. After students have circled their answers, reread the passage orally, and have them give their answers to the questions. Discuss/explain all the answers, paying special attention to the inference questions and to tricky "distractors" (as in item 1, answer *a*).

46

Dear Dot

Dear Dot—

I am sixteen years old but very mature for my age. I am dating a twenty-three-year-old man. We enjoy each other's company but my parents are very much against our relationship. They say that Darrel is too old for me and that I should date boys my own age. I find boys my age boring and immature. I enjoy my relationship with Darrel and I don't want to give him up. How can I get my parents to leave me alone?

Sophisticated Lady

Discuss each of the questions in class. Then write your answers.

1. What do the words *mature* and *immature* mean in this letter? _____
   _____

2. Do you think it is O.K. for a sixteen-year-old to date a twenty-three-year-old? Why or why not? _____
   _____
   _____

3. Should parents have the right to approve or disapprove of their teenage children's dates? Why or why not? _____
   _____
   _____

4. How can Sophisticated Lady work out a compromise with her parents? _____

Write About It

Now put yourself in Dot's place. Write a helpful answer to Sophisticated Lady. Remember, you want to help solve her problem, not make fun of the writer or criticize her.

Dear Sophisticated Lady—

_____
_____
_____
_____
_____
_____
_____
_____

Active and Passive

Sentences in the *active voice* put the emphasis on the doer. "José ate the beans" is in the active voice. Sentences in the passive voice change the emphasis. "The beans were eaten by José" is in the passive voice. The emphasis is on the beans, rather than on José. The passive voice is formed using the appropriate form of the verb *to be* and the past participle of the main verb. In the example above, the active voice verb was in the past tense ("ate"), so the verb *to be* is in the past tense ("were") when the sentence is changed to the passive. The passive voice is formed the same way in the present, past, future, and present perfect tenses. In each case, the tense of the verb *to be* in the passive sentence matches the tense of the main verb in the active sentence. Look at the examples below.

Active	**Passive**
William Shakespeare wrote *Hamlet*.	*Hamlet* was written by William Shakespeare.
People in Lebanon eat tabouli.	Tabouli is eaten in Lebanon.
The police have arrested Tom.	Tom has been arrested by the police.

A. **Complete each of the passive sentences with one of the words from the Data Bank.** The first one is done for you.

1. Portuguese is ___*spoken*___ in Brazil.

2. Many stars are _____ only by astronomers.

3. President Bush was _____ at Yale University in Connecticut.

4. The Statue of Liberty was _____ to the United States by France.

5. The book *War and Peace* was _____ by Leo Tolstoy.

6. The *Mona Lisa* and *The Last Supper* were _____ by Leonardo da Vinci.

7. The electric light bulb was _____ by Thomas Edison.

8. The mail was _____ very late yesterday.

D A T A B A N K

written   delivered   educated   given   invented   painted   seen   spoken

---

B. **Complete each of the following sentences by using the correct form of the verb *to be* and the past participle of the verb in parentheses.** The first one is done for you.

(grow) 1. Coffee ___*is*___ ___*grown*___ in Brazil.

(make) 2. My shoes _____ _____ in Italy.

(publish) 3. This book _____ _____ by Addison-Wesley.

(cook) 4. The dinner _____ _____ too long, and it burned.

(steal) 5. $50,000 _____ _____ from the bank.

(see) 6. The accident _____ _____ by many witnesses.

(sell) 7. Tools _____ _____ at hardware stores.

(make) 8. My shirt _____ _____ of cotton.

Skill Objectives: Forming and using the passive voice; distinguishing between active and passive. Read the introductory paragraph with the class, emphasizing the use and formation of the passive. Do the examples and ask volunteers for others. *Part A:* Do items 1 and 2 orally, then assign as written work. *Part B:* Call attention to the verbs in parentheses. Do items 1, 2, and 3 orally, then assign as written work. When students have finished, go over answers with the class to check understanding.

Who, What, When

A. Match the two columns by writing the letter of the correct name or names next to the item in the first column that it goes with. Use an encyclopedia if you need to. The first one is done for you.

_g_ 1. The pyramids were built 4,000 years ago

_____ 2. Gaul was conquered in 51 B.C.

_____ 3. Rome was conquered in A.D. 455

_____ 4. England was invaded in A.D. 1066

_____ 5. The Crusades were started in 1147

_____ 6. The Magna Carta was signed in 1215

_____ 7. Europe was devastated in 1348

_____ 8. The *Mona Lisa* was painted in 1400

_____ 9. The movable type printing press was invented in 1454

_____ 10. The New World was discovered in 1492

_____ 11. The Sistine Chapel was painted in 1512

_____ 12. The mercury thermometer was invented in 1714

_____ 13. *Romeo and Juliet* was written in 1596

_____ 14. The Declaration of Independence was written in 1776

_____ 15. The Choral or Ninth Symphony was composed in 1824

_____ 16. Abraham Lincoln was assassinated in 1865

_____ 17. The phonograph was invented in 1877

_____ 18. The first airplane was flown in 1903

_____ 19. The world of physics was revolutionized in 1915

_____ 20. Penicillin was discovered in 1928

_____ 21. *Gone with the Wind* was written in 1936

_____ 22. The helicopter was invented in 1939

_____ 23. The Polaroid camera was invented in 1948

a. by the Wright brothers.

b. by Ludwig van Beethoven.

c. by Albert Einstein.

d. by Michelangelo.

e. by Thomas Edison.

f. by John Wilkes Booth.

g. by the Egyptians.

h. by Thomas Jefferson.

i. by Dr. Alexander Fleming.

j. by Gabriel Fahrenheit.

k. by Julius Caesar.

l. by King John.

m. by William Shakespeare.

n. by Edwin Land.

o. by Pope Urban II.

p. by Johann Gutenberg.

q. by Igor Sikorsky.

r. by Leonardo da Vinci.

s. by Christopher Columbus.

t. by Margaret Mitchell.

u. by the bubonic plague.

v. by William the Conquerer.

w. by the Vandals.

B. Check your work with your teacher. Then rewrite each sentence on your paper using the active voice. For example: The Egyptians built the pyramids 4,000 years ago.

Skill Objectives: Understanding the passive voice; using reference books; placing historical events in time. *Part A:* Do the first three items with the group; discuss how they can find answers if they do not know them (review the use of the encyclopedia). Assign as independent work. Check answers in class when students have finished. *Part B:* Do the first three sentences orally, then assign as written work. Extension: Have each student choose one of the items and write an essay about it.

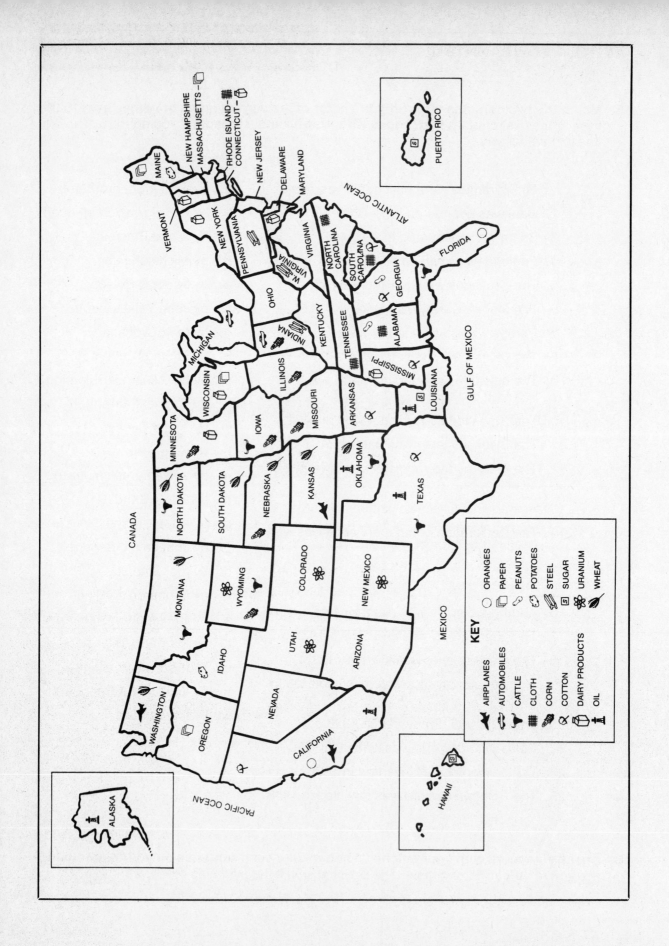

50

Where Is It Made or Grown?

The map on the previous page shows some of the products of some of the states in the United States. **Use the map and its "key" to answer the following questions. Use complete sentences.** The first one is done for you.

1. In what two states are automobiles made? *Automobiles are made in Michigan and Indiana.*

2. In what states are oranges grown? _____

3. Where is corn grown? _____

4. Where are airplanes made? _____

5. Where is cloth woven? _____

6. Where is steel produced? _____

7. Where are potatoes grown? _____

8. Where is oil found? _____

9. Where are cattle raised? _____

10. Where is sugar produced? _____

11. Where are dairy products made? _____

12. Where is paper manufactured? _____

13. Where is cotton grown? _____

14. Where is uranium found? _____

15. Where is wheat grown? _____

16. Where are peanuts grown? _____

Skill Objectives: Interpreting a map with product symbols; forming and using the passive voice. Discuss the map on page 50. Call attention to the key, and elicit that the symbols on the map show where different products come from. Be sure students understand such terms as *cattle* and *dairy products*. Point out that the map shows the principal products of states and the principal states that produce them, not all products and all producers. Go over the first five items orally, then assign as written work.

Getting Your License

In the United States, you are not allowed to drive a car unless you have a driver's license. Each state sets the rules for getting a license in that state. As a result, the rules vary somewhat from state to state. The statements below apply to many states, but remember that your own state may have somewhat different rules and policies. **Read the article, then answer the questions.**

To get a driver's license, all states require that you be above a certain age, that you know how to drive, and that you know about traffic laws and safety rules.

Age. In most states, you have to be at least sixteen years old to start learning to drive. Anyone younger than that who is behind the wheel of a moving car is violating the law, even if he or she is closely supervised. Age sixteen is also the minimum age in most states for taking driver's education courses in schools.

Driver's Education and Learner Permits. Driver's education courses begin with classroom instruction on the rules of the road and traffic laws. You learn, for example, how fast it is safe to go in certain areas, what to do if a fire engine is near, and what the different road signs mean. When you finish the classroom course, you can apply for a Learner's Permit. In some states you have to take a test before you receive the permit.

When you have your Learner's Permit, you are allowed to drive a car under supervision. This means that you can drive only when you are accompanied by a licensed driver. It is during this period that you actually learn to drive. You learn to steer the car, to start it, to shift gears (if the car you will drive has a manual shift), to pass other cars, to park, and all the other practical things you will need to know.

Your Learner's Permit is good for only a limited amount of time, since it is expected that you will be ready to take the test for your license after a relatively short period of instruction.

Tests. When you think you are ready to get your license, you fill out an application to take the driver's tests.

The tests vary from one state to another, but in general you will be tested for vision, for knowledge of road signs and pavement markings, for understanding of traffic and safety rules, and for driving ability. You take the road test only if you have passed all the other tests.

Most people prefer to take the road test in the same car in which they have been learning. That way, they don't have to get used to an unfamiliar car. During the test, the driving examiner sees how well you can drive and whether you obey all the traffic laws. If you pass the test, you get your license (or a temporary one) immediately.

Languages. In some states, driver's tests are given in languages other than English. Remember, though, that most road signs are only in English.

Identification. When you apply for your license test, you will need to bring identification showing your address in your state. You may also have to have your Social Security number on your application. If you don't have a Social Security number, you will have to get one. Some states may require a birth certificate or other proof of your age.

New Residents. If you move to a new state, you will have to get a new license in that state, but you may not have to take a new road test if you already have a license from another state. You probably will, however, have to take a vision test and a test about the state's traffic laws and road signs.

(Go on to the next page)

Skill Objectives: Reading for main idea and details; applying personal experience to interpretation of reading materials. Read the introductory paragraph with the class. Emphasize that states vary in the rules and procedures for licensing drivers. Ask if any students have licenses or are in the process of getting them. As students read the article, ask them to think about how the procedure in your state differs from the one described and how it is the same. After the reading, discuss these questions with the class.

52

A. What are the steps you need to take to get a driver's license? Put the following statements in chronological order, 1, 2, 3, 4, 5, etc.

_____ Make an appointment for a driver's (road) test.

_____ Attend driver education class either in high school or at a private auto school.

_____ Take vision test.

_____ Fill out a form for a Learner's Permit.

_____ Take road test.

_____ Begin actual driving instruction accompanied by a licensed driver.

_____ Get license.

B. Read each of these statements. Decide if it is true or false. If it is true, circle the _T._ If it is false, circle the _F._

T F   1. You must take a hearing test to get your driver's license.

T F   2. When you complete classroom instruction, you can apply for a driver's license.

T F   3. A person with a Learner's Permit can drive only with another person in the car.

T F   4. The rules for getting a license are set by the federal government in Washington, D.C.

T F   5. In most states, you must be at least 16 to start driver's education courses.

T F   6. The classroom instruction sessions are where you actually learn to drive.

T F   7. A Learner's Permit is good for only a limited time.

T F   8. The road test is usually given before the other driver's tests.

T F   9. The examiner in the road test is interested not only in how well you drive the car but also in how well you obey traffic rules.

T F   10. You get a license immediately after you have passed the tests.

T F   11. Driver's tests are given only in English because this is the language of road signs.

T F   12. Some states require a Social Security number on a license application.

T F   13. All states ask that you bring a birth certificate with you when you apply for a license.

T F   14. If you move from New York to Ohio, you have to get a new license in Ohio.

T F   15. If you already have a license in one state, you will not need to take any tests to get one in another state.

C. On your paper, write a paragraph about why getting a driver's license is so important to most teenagers and young adults.

Skill Objectives: Sequencing; reading for details; expressing opinions in writing. _Part A:_ Read the instructions with the class, then ask which of the sentences should be number 1 (attend driver education class). Assign the remainder of the exercise as written work. _Part B:_ Tell students they are to decide whether each statement is true or false _according to the article on page 52._ They may refer to the article as often as they wish. Do the first three items orally, then assign as written work. _Part C:_ Lead a discussion about the importance to young people of getting a driver's license. Then assign the paragraph as independent written work, perhaps as homework.

53

Reading the Newspaper: Automobiles

Millions and millions of automobiles are sold in the United States every year. Nearly every daily newspaper prints advertisements for cars. Some of these are ads that promote a particular make of car, such as Ford, Chevrolet, Chrysler, Subaru, Toyota, Honda, Nissan, or Volvo. Some are ads placed by car dealers. And some are ads placed by individual people who want to sell their old cars.

A. Look at the advertisement below for a new car. Then answer the questions. Use complete sentences. The first question is answered for you. Answer the others on your paper.

6.9% FINANCING
Annual Percentage Rate

24,000 MILE — 24 MONTH WARRANTY

4 SPEED
FUEL INJECTION
4 CYL. ENGINE
FRONT WHEEL DRIVE
INDEPENDENT
SUSPENSION

52 M.P.G. HWY
37 E.P.A.

$9983
113 in Stock
IMMEDIATE DELIVERY

$358.03 PER MONTH
$2000.00 DOWN

BUILT IN AMERICA
Cash price $358.03 per mo. Down Payment $2000.00
Annual percentage rate 6.9 for 48 months with bank
approved credit. Amount financed $7983. Interest $609.72.
Deferred payment price $10,592.
Total of payments $8592.72

---

1. How many miles is this car warranted (guaranteed) for? _____ *This car is warranted for 24,000 miles.*

2. How many months is it warranted for?
3. If the whole price of the car is paid at the time it is bought, how much is paid?
4. If the car is financed (money is borrowed for it), how much money is asked for at the time the car is bought?
5. How much is paid each month?
6. What features of the car are mentioned in the ad?
7. How much interest is paid on the loan?
8. How many cars does the dealer have in stock?
9. Where is this car built?

Skill Objectives: Interpreting advertisements; reading for details; building vocabulary. Ask students if any of them own cars. How did they (or parents or friends) get their cars? Did they buy them through a newspaper ad? Tell students they will be studying some ads for cars. Read (or have students read) the introductory paragraphs. *Part A:* Have students read the advertisement, then use it to answer the questions. Do some or all questions orally, then assign as written work.

B. Look at these ads for used cars. You can buy a used car from a dealer or from the owner of the car. Dealers have to give you a guarantee, although it is usually for a short period. If you buy from an individual, be careful. Not all states have laws to protect you! Be sure you know what the condition of the car is. It is a good idea to take it to a mechanic you trust and have this person inspect the car before you buy it.

On your paper, answer the questions about the ads. Use complete sentences.

CHEVROLET station wagon, 1984, power brakes & steering, air cond., auto. trans., runs well. $3200. Call 784-2114 after 6 or weekends.

'85 WHITE FORD ESCORT, 4 cylinder, standard, 4 good tires & 2 snows. Some rot. Driven daily. Reliable, cheap transportation. $2200. Call 963-5164 after 4.

'88 MERCURY BOBCAT 46,000 miles, economical 4 cylinder, 4-speed, hatchback. Sharp car in mint cond. $4195. Moreno Motors, Rte. 6, Whitman at Dickinson line. Over a decade of fair dealing. 447-2130.

TOYOTA CELICA GT Liftback, 1987, original owner. 57,000 miles. In perfect cond. Excellent maintenance experience. Best offer. 227-5612.

1989 NISSAN B210, mint cond. 26,000 miles. AM-FM stereo, 4 speed standard transmission. Excellent gas mileage. $7995. Galaxy Nissan, Dale St., Wenford. 919-8980.

1983 VOLKSWAGEN Good shape. $1,000 or best offer. 871-1421.

1. Four of the cars are advertised for sale by their owners, and two by dealers. Which two cars are advertised by car dealers?

2. What is a station wagon? A hatchback? A liftback?

3. Which cars have 4-speed transmission? Which car has automatic transmission?

4. "Mint condition" means excellent condition. Which cars are in mint condition?

5. You are looking for a car that costs no more than $1,000. Which cars will you *not* look at?

6. Which car has a stereo radio? Which one has air conditioning?

7. Your state has a sales tax of 4%. How much sales tax do you have to pay on the Ford Escort?

8. All the ads give the year and make of the car. What other information do all the ads give?

9. What does "best offer" mean?

10. How old is the Toyota Celica?

C. Write a description of your car or the car you would like to own. Tell as much as you can about it. Tell what make it is, what year, what color. Tell how many cylinders it has, what kind of transmission, and what kind of radio. What special features does your car have? What do you like most about it? Why?

D. Imagine that you are going to sell the car you have described. Write an advertisement for it that will make people want to buy it. You are limited to 6 lines with no more than 38 letters and spaces in a line. Remember that your ad must include your telephone number or address.

Skill Objectives: Interpreting advertisements; reading for details; writing descriptions; writing advertisements. The ad on page 54 is for a new car. Most young people buy used cars, however. This page deals with used cars. *Part A*: Discuss advantages and disadvantages of buying from a dealer and an owner. Have students read the ads. Go over the questions orally, then assign as written work. *Parts C and D*: Discuss both activities in class before students write. You may wish to assign these as homework.

Restating Information

You can often express an idea in either of two ways. You can use the active voice or you can use the passive voice. Look at these sentences:

Rosa directed the class play.
The class play was directed by Rosa.

Binh will pay for our lunch.
Our lunch will be paid for by Binh.

Both sentences convey the same information. It is important to be able to express and understand ideas in both ways.

Look at the sentences below. Choose the sentence in the active voice that best expresses the idea of the sentence in the passive voice. Make sure that the tense remains the same in active and passive voice sentences.

1. The fish were caught by the boys at the river.
   a. The boys are catching fish at the river.
   b. The boys caught the fish at the river.
   c. The river was catching fish for the boys.

2. The tests are given by the professors every Saturday.
   a. The professors gave the test every Saturday.
   b. Every Saturday the tests give the professors.
   c. Every Saturday the professors give the tests.

3. You will be greeted at the airport by a man in a blue suit.
   a. You will greet a man in a blue suit at the airport.
   b. A man in a blue suit was greeted at the airport by you.
   c. A man in a blue suit will greet you at the airport.

4. Julie was given those earrings by her grandmother.
   a. Julie's grandmother gave her those earrings.
   b. Julie's grandmother was given those earrings by her.
   c. Julie's grandmother gives her those earrings.

5. Independence Day is celebrated on July 4th by Americans.
   a. Americans celebrated Independence Day on July 4th.
   b. Americans celebrate Independence Day on July 4th.
   c. July 4th celebrates Americans on Independence Day.

6. The winner was chosen at random by the judges.
   a. The winner chose the judges at random.
   b. The judges chose the winner at random.
   c. The judges will choose a winner at random.

7. I don't have my homework because it was eaten by my dog.
   a. The teacher didn't give homework so my dog didn't eat it.
   b. I don't feed my dog my homework but I don't have it.
   c. My dog ate my homework so I can't pass it in.

8. The flowers will be planted in the school garden by the students in Room 212.
   a. The students from Room 212 will plant flowers.
   b. The students in Room 212 picked the flowers.
   c. The students planted the flowers in Room 212.

9. The winner's national anthem is played when the Olympic medal is awarded.
   a. The winner plays the national anthem for the Olympic award.
   b. They play the winner's national anthem when they award the Olympic medal.
   c. The Olympic medal plays the winner's national anthem as an award.

Skill Objectives: Simplifying and restating information; understanding active and passive voice. Review the meaning of active and passive voice. Explain that the passive voice has tenses just as the active voice does (many students think all passives are past tense). Read the explanation in the box at the top of the page and make sure that all students understand that the two sentences in each pair convey the same meaning. Do item 1 as a class, then assign the page for independent work. Review all answers in class. After students have completed the exercise, have them generate their own sentences and change active ones to passive and passive ones to active.

Dear Dot

Dear Dot—

My oldest sister was killed in a car accident when she was nineteen years old. Now my parents say I can't get my license until my 21st birthday. My parents think that they are protecting me, but actually, they are doing the opposite. I am forced to ride with kids who are less responsible than I am. I am being deprived of driving experience, and I am also being deprived of dating experiences. Many girls refuse to date a guy nowadays unless he has a car. How can I make my parents change their minds? When I bring the subject up, my father yells at me and my mother cries.

Carless in Arlington

Discuss each of the questions in class. Then write your answers.

1. Is Carless's parents' decision an emotional one or a logical one? How do you know? What is the difference between these kinds of decisions? _____
_____

2. Does Carless make a good argument for having his license? Why or why not? _____
_____

3. Do you think his parents will be able to understand his need? Why or why not? _____
_____

4. Do you think peace in a family is more important than one individual's needs? Explain your answer. _____
_____

Write About It

Now put yourself in Dot's place. Write a helpful answer to Carless. Remember, you want to help him solve his problem, not make fun of him or criticize him. Use more paper if you need to.

Dear Carless—

_____

_____

_____

_____

_____

_____

_____

_____

Skill Objectives: Reading for main idea; reasoning deductively; making judgments; expressing opinions in writing. Have students read the letter. Discuss each question in class, with special attention to the first and fourth. Encourage free expression of opinion, but be sure opinions are supported. Then have students write answers to the questions (they may need extra paper). Suggest they use these answers as the basis for their letters. You may wish to assign the letter-writing activity as homework.

Americana

How much do you know about things that are American? **Try this quiz. Circle your answers. After you have completed the quiz, discuss the answers in class.** The first item is done for you.

1. Broadway is famous as the home of _____.
   a. concerts   b. hotels   (c. plays)   d. sports

2. The state famous for oil wells and Dallas is _____.
   a. Ohio   b. New York   c. Texas   d. California

3. Standing under the mistletoe can get you a _____.
   a. kiss   b. flower   c. cake   d. slap

4. Mark Twain is a famous American _____.
   a. singer   b. dancer   c. showman   d. author

5. The Exxon company is a large producer of _____.
   a. meat   b. sugar   c. coffee   d. gasoline

6. Abraham Lincoln is on the _____ bill.
   a. $5   b. $10   c. $1   d. $100

7. You go to the World Series to see _____.
   a. hockey   b. basketball   c. baseball   d. football

8. The car which is not American of the following is _____.
   a. Ford   b. Chevrolet   c. Pontiac   d. Jaguar

9. A Polaroid is a _____.
   a. star   b. computer   c. food   d. camera

10. You would most likely see the letters Rx in front of _____.
    a. schools   b. government buildings   c. drugstores   d. key shops

11. A Twinkie is a kind of _____.
    a. fish   b. star   c. cake   d. candy

12. One-A-Day is a famous _____.
    a. calendar   b. TV show   c. book   d. vitamin

13. Presley, Parton, and Wonder are famous _____.
    a. singers   b. lawyers   c. cars   d. shoes

14. Hershey Company is famous for its _____.
    a. chocolate   b. donuts   c. sugar   d. hams

15. BLT is a name for a _____.
    a. margarine   b. pie maker   c. TV network   d. sandwich

16. Campbell's is famous for _____.
    a. tents   b. candy   c. soup   d. appliances.

17. The country is split into East and West by the _____.
    a. White Mountains   b. Mississippi   c. border   d. Red River

18. Maxwell House is a famous kind of _____.
    a. coffee   b. hotel   c. restaurant   d. cake

19. The favorite food eaten at baseball games is _____.
    a. hamburgers   b. steak   c. hot dogs   d. pizza

20. The national bird of the U.S. is _____.
    a. the robin   b. the eagle   c. the turkey   d. the bluebird

Skill Objectives: Building vocabulary; understanding American culture; taking multiple-choice tests. Tell the class that this page asks about many kinds of "things that are American." Point out that most students probably will not know the answers to many items, but that this is a chance to find out, since you will be discussing all the items after students have done the quiz. Stress that they should read all four choices before marking an answer; tell them to guess if they are not sure.

Analogies

An analogy is a comparison between two sets of words. Look at the example below. Which word completes the second set of words in a way that matches the first set of words?

hot : cold : : wet : _____   (You say: "Hot is to cold as wet is to _____")
water   dry   swim   warm

Clue: Put the first two words into a sentence that shows how those words fit together. "The opposite of *hot* is *cold.*" Then substitute the second set of words into the same sentence:
"The opposite of *wet* is _____ .

Now complete each of the following analogies. Circle your answers.

1. nickel : five : : dime : _____
   money   ten   dollar   one

2. puppy : dog : : colt : _____
   kitten   horse   calf   tiger

3. green : grass : : white : _____
   snow   winter   tree   black

4. twelve : dozen : : two : _____
   doesn't   eggs   pair   eyes

5. hot : melt : : cold : _____
   break   winter   heat   freeze

6. Thanksgiving : Thursday : : Easter : _____
   spring   Sunday   vacation   April

7. write : written : : swim : _____
   wrote   swam   swum   swimming

8. four : even : : seven : _____
   nine   eleven   odd   number

9. thief : robber : : murderer : _____
   killer   crime   steal   gun

10. author : book : : painter : _____
    museum   artist   brushes   picture

11. mouse : mice : : tooth : _____
    mouth   teeth   bite   tithe

12. question : answer : : ask : _____
    reply   sentence   want   period

13. "post" : after : : "pre" : _____
    soon   preview   before   again

14. watch : wrist : : ring : _____
    look   finger   hand   bell

15. soldier : army : : player : _____
    war   team   game   score

16. states : country : : teams : _____
    league   sports   athletes   Olympics

17. play : acts : : book : _____
    pretends   fiction   words   chapters

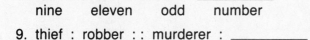
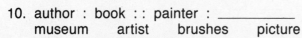

Skill Objectives: Classifying words; reasoning logically; discovering relationships; building vocabulary. Discuss the concept of an analogy. Emphasize that the first two words may be related in any one of a number of different ways, and that the second two words must have the same relationship to each other as the first two. Go over the example and the clue; be sure students understand the idea. Do the first four items orally; have students name the relationship each time. Then assign as written work. Extension: Have students write five analogies of their own.

What Will Happen . . .?

When you talk about something that may happen in the future, use the present tense in the first part of the sentence, and *will* or *may* in the second part.

If the boy *steps* on the banana peel, he *will* slip.
If the girl *falls* off her bike, she *may* get hurt.

Study the picture, then complete the sentences below.

1. If the man falls from the ladder, _____.

2. If the dog escapes from its leash, _____.

3. If the woman walks under the ladder, _____.

4. If the boy runs after the ball, _____.

5. If the boy doesn't run after the ball, _____.

6. If the car drives through the puddle, _____.

7. If the black cat walks in front of the man, _____.

8. If the bus stops, _____.

9. If the bus doesn't stop, _____.

10. If it rains, _____.

Skill Objectives: Understanding cause and effect; using conditionals; expressing future action with *will* and *may*. Have students study the picture; review the various pictured situations orally and identify the actions. Read (or have a student read) the introductory paragraph; discuss the difference in meaning between *will* and *may*. Be sure students understand the sequence of tenses, then assign the questions as written work.

If You Forget

A. Answer the following questions.

1. If you forget to put ice cream in the freezer, what will happen? _____

   _____

2. If you drive too fast, what may happen? _____

   _____

3. If you mix red and yellow paint, what color will you have? _____

   _____

4. If it is raining and the temperature drops below 32°, what will happen? _____

   _____

5. If you forget to take back your library book when it is due, what will happen? _____

   _____

6. If you forget to pay the electric bill for two months, what may happen? _____

   _____

B. Finish the sentences below. The first one is done for you.

1. If I leave my car windows open, *the seats may get wet.* _____.

2. If they don't study for the test, _____.

3. If you eat too much candy, _____.

4. If Mary doesn't stop smoking, _____.

5. If you don't come to class on time, _____.

6. I'll bring my umbrella to school tomorrow if _____.

7. I'll lend you my car if _____.

8. Paul will have bad luck if _____.

9. You will lose weight if _____.

10. Carla won't pass the test if _____.

Skill Objectives: Understanding cause and effect; predicting outcomes; completing conditional sentences. *Part A:* Make sure students understand that the modals in the question should be repeated in the answer. Do all or some of the questions orally; try to get as many different answers to each question as possible. Assign as written work. *Part B:* Discuss why *may* is better than *will* in the first answer, then have students do the first five. Do questions 6 and 7 orally, eliciting different answers, then assign.

61

Could You Please Tell Me . . . ?

> Questions often start with phrases such as the following:
>
> Do you know . . . ?   Could you please tell me . . . ?
> Can you tell me . . . ?   Do you have any idea . . . ?
>
> Example: Where *is* Payton University?
> *Can you tell me* where Payton University *is*?
>
> Example: When *did* the movie *start*?
> *Could you please tell me* when the movie *started*?

Look at each question below. Change it to start with the polite phrase on the line. Notice that when you do this, the order of the words in the question is changed. Use the examples in the box as models for your answers.

1. How old is the President of the United States?

   Do you know _____

2. How much does a pack of gum cost?

   Can you tell me _____

3. When will the next bus arrive?

   Could you please tell me _____

4. Where did my mother go?

   Do you know _____

5. Where are my keys?

   Do you have any idea _____

6. How did that package get here?

   Can you tell me _____

7. What was our homework assignment?

   Could you please tell me _____

8. Where will the test be given?

   Can you tell me _____

9. How long has that woman been waiting?

   Do you have any idea _____

10. How has the weather been in Florida?

    Do you know _____

Skill Objectives: Writing questions with polite introductory phrases; using correct word order. Lead a general discussion about manners and politeness. Why are they important? What purpose do they serve? Explain that certain phrases are used in English to show politeness, and read the examples at the top of the page. Elicit that the word order of the question is changed when the polite phrase is used. Then assign the page as written work.

Trivia Time

Work in groups of three or four to agree on answers to these questions. The group that can answer the most questions correctly wins. Use the lines to write your answers. Use short answers.

A.
1. When did Americans first land on the moon? _____
2. Who is the principal/director/head of this school? _____
3. How old must you be to vote in the United States? _____
4. In what state(s) are cars made in the United States? _____
5. What is a "whopper junior"? _____
6. About how many people are there in this city/town? _____
7. What holiday do Americans celebrate in July? _____
8. When was the last big earthquake in California? _____
9. What does "awesome" mean? _____
10. How many 25¢ stamps are there in a dozen? _____
11. How many months have 28 days in them? _____
12. Who created Mickey Mouse and Donald Duck? _____
13. What did Thomas Edison invent? _____
14. Where is the Golden Gate? _____
15. What was the "Mayflower"? _____

B. Answer yes or no.
1. Is 16 the age people can get a driver's license in this state? _____
2. Could women vote in all states in the United States before 1920? _____
3. Have many Asians come to the United States in the past ten years? _____
4. Is there a war anywhere in the world at this time? _____
5. Were Americans the first to travel in space? _____
6. Is coffee grown in the United States? _____
7. Did Columbus discover America in 1942? _____
8. Is George Bush the President of the United States now? _____
9. Does February have only 28 days every year? _____
10. Was the Statue of Liberty given to the United States by France? _____
11. Does sound travel faster than light? _____
12. Is Boston farther north than Washington, D.C.? _____
13. Is Portuguese spoken in Brazil? _____
14. Is the Great Barrier Reef in Hawaii? _____
15. Did Peter Cooper invent the electric light? _____

Skill Objectives: Reviewing/understanding cultural and historical information in a game situation. *Part A:* Divide the class into small groups, trying to balance abilities between and within groups. When students have finished (no time limit), go around each group and quietly record answers. Announce the winning group. Go over answers with the class. (You may want to create your own set of questions that are more appropriate to your class.) *Part B:* Do Part B as a class in another game situation, or assign it as written work. Again check the answers with the entire class. As an extension, you may wish to teach students how to answer if they don't know: "I don't know *when Americans first landed on the moon*." "I don't know *if Americans were the first to travel in space*."

Reading The Newspaper: The Editorial Page

News articles try to present only *facts*. The editorial page is the section of the newspaper where news writers are given the opportunity to express their *opinions* about recent events, policies, trends and community activities. Read the editorial below, then answer the questions.

THE TELEVISION HABIT

It is time for responsible parents to pull the plug on television. Ninety percent of television programs shown today are a waste of time and an offense to any intelligent person, adult or child. People must begin to say *no* to television, to refuse to let it interfere with their lives. They must find other hobbies and pastimes. Televisions across the country must be turned off.

It is estimated that most children watch three to five hours of television per day. Imagine the amount of constructive work that could be done in this time—the books that could be read, the chores that could be done—it staggers the mind. Yet, across the nation, parents continue to allow their children free access to television. Test scores are plunging and the rate of functional illiteracy is increasing, but nothing is done.

Turning off the television and forcing children to account for their free time is the first step in changing a wasteful national habit.

A. Answer these questions with complete sentences.

1. What is the writer's opinion of television? _____

   _____

   _____

2. What fact does the writer give about the TV viewing habits of American children? ____

   _____

   _____

3. What does the phrase "functional illiteracy" mean? _____

   _____

   _____

4. What does the author think is the reason that test scores have plunged and the level of

   high school literacy has become lower? _____

   _____

5. Is this an opinion or a fact? _____

6. Which phrase best describes the tone of the editorial (the author's attitude or feelings

   towards the subject)?

   a. light-hearted, humorous   b. forceful and demanding

   c. calm and reasonable   d. willing to compromise

Skill Objectives: Distinguishing between fact and opinion; making inferences; reading for detail; establishing tone. Read (or have a student read) the introductory paragraph and discuss what an editorial is. Then have students read the editorial silently. *Part A:* Assign the first five questions. Then discuss the idea of "tone," and read the editorial aloud in a "forceful and demanding" manner; assign the sixth question. *Extension:* Have students read other editorials (they may bring them in) and establish their tone.

B. The editorial page also contains "Letters to the Editor." These letters are written by people in the community. The letters may comment on local or national events and trends, or they may respond to previous editorials or letters to the editor.

Letters to the editor are written to express an opinion. The writer usually includes certain facts that support his or her viewpoint. Look at the statements below about television viewing in the U.S. Some of the statements are facts and some are opinions. **Write F in front of each fact, and O in front of each opinion.**

Statements About U.S. Television Viewing

_____ 1. TV has broadened people's experiences and enriched their lives.

_____ 2. Without TV, most Americans would never see the President speak or watch a major league ball game, or learn about wild animals by seeing them in their native environment.

_____ 3. In the average American home, at least one TV set is on for six hours every day.

_____ 4. Television shows present an unrealistic picture of American life.

_____ 5. Television keeps elderly people young at heart and interested in life by keeping them informed about world events and involving them in the problems and feelings of TV characters.

_____ 6. The average American child spends more time sitting and watching TV than in any other single waking activity.

_____ 7. Every television set is equipped with an ON/OFF switch.

_____ 8. Violence is common on many TV shows, but particularly in cartoons geared to children.

_____ 9. Watching violent programs on TV causes people to act more violently.

_____ 10. Educational TV programs have successfully taught many children early reading and number skills in an entertaining way.

C. **Now, write a letter to the editor responding to "The Television Habit."** You may agree or disagree with the editorial. You may bring up other sides of the issue. You may want to tell what points of the editorial you particularly agree or disagree with. Your letter should contain both opinions and facts. Include only those facts that support your opinion.

Dear Editor:

_____

_____

_____

_____

_____

_____

_____

_____

_____

_____

_____

Skill Objectives: Distinguishing between fact and opinion; expressing and supporting an opinion in writing. *Part B:* Do the first three items orally, reviewing the difference between fact and opinion. Then assign as written work. *Part C:* Suggest that students use material from Part B for their letters if they wish to. Read the instructions and discuss the kinds of things students will include in their letters. Then assign, perhaps as homework. Extension: Bring in and analyze letters to the editor.

65

Saying It Another Way

It is important to be able to understand different ways of asking questions or expressing ideas. The exercise below will give you practice in restating questions.

Circle the sentence that is most similar in meaning to the numbered one.

1. Would you mind if I borrowed your notes?
   a. Lend me your notes, please.
   b. I borrowed your notes.
   c. I minded your notes.
   d. Can I lend you my notes?

2. Could you tell me where the theater is located?
   a. I don't want to know where the theater is.
   b. Where is the theater, please?
   c. Please give me directions to the library.
   d. When will you be going to the theater?

3. Do you know when the next plane will be departing?
   a. Has the next plane arrived yet?
   b. What time is the next plane scheduled to take off?
   c. When did the plane depart?
   d. I can't take off on the next plane because I'm not packed.

4. Do you have any idea what the weather will be like tonight?
   a. You can never be sure about the weather.
   b. Doesn't anyone like the weather we are having tonight?
   c. Do you like this weather?
   d. Do you know anything about tonight's weather forecast?

5. Would it be all right if I gave you some advice?
   a. Would you like my opinion?
   b. Would you give me some advice about my problems?
   c. Would it be all right if I took your advice?
   d. I should have listened to your advice.

6. You don't mind if I come along to the dance, do you?
   a. You don't want me to dance with you.
   b. Is it okay if I come to the dance with you?
   c. You're out of your mind if you expect me to dance.
   d. I hope you don't mind, but I can't go to the dance.

7. Could you explain why so many people are afraid of mice?
   a. I'm trying to explain why mice frighten me.
   b. I don't understand why mice frighen me.
   c. I don't understand why mice frighten so many people.
   d. Most people aren't afraid of mice, are they?

Skill Objectives: Simplifying and restating information; understanding different levels of discourse; understanding various question forms. Explain that sometimes in formal situations, a more "polite" form of English is customary, especially in asking questions or seeking permission. In each item, the numbered question is in the polite, formal form. Students are to find the other sentence that says the same thing. You may wish to do one or two items orally as a class before assigning the page for independent written work.

Fact or Opinion

FACTS are true statements that can be checked and proven. OPINIONS are what a person thinks or feels about something.

A. Read each sentence below and decide if it states a fact or an opinion. Write *F* after each FACT, and *O* after each OPINION.

1. April 15 is the deadline for some federal tax payments. ____

2. Water freezes at 32° Fahrenheit. ____

3. You can never be too rich or too thin. ____

4. Nothing is more important than your health. ____

5. Beethoven was the greatest musical composer who ever lived. ____

6. Many words in English have Latin roots. ____

7. The pyramids are early civilization's greatest accomplishment. ____

8. There are 206 bones in the human skeleton. ____

9. The Chinese alphabet has over 3,000 characters. ____

10. Early to bed, early to rise, makes a man healthy, wealthy, and wise. ____

11. Rock music is for teenagers only. ____

12. Odd numbers are numbers that can't be divided by 2. ____

13. Neil Armstrong walked on the moon in 1969. ____

14. Panda bears are native to China. ____

15. Everyone should have a college education. ____

16. You can't teach an old dog new tricks. ____

17. The sun is a small star compared to many others in the sky. ____

18. A prime number can only be divided by 1 and itself. ____

19. There is no life in outer space. ____

20. Plane travel is the most efficient means of transportation. ____

21. The medical profession is the most noble. ____

22. Pluto is the planet most distant from the sun. ____

23. It's important for young children to play musical instruments. ____

24. You can't judge a book by its cover. ____

25. Christopher Columbus was born in Genoa, Italy. ____

B. Find an *opinion* on this page that you agree with. Then, on your own paper, write a paragraph of five or six sentences that supports the opinion. Start your paragraph with "I think . . ." or "My opinion is . . ." and tell why you agree with the opinion.

Skill Objective: Distinguishing between fact and opinion. *Part A:* Make sure students understand that this is not a true/false exercise. Point out that all the statements are either factually true or true as the opinions of some person or persons; the student must decide which. Point out that some of the statements are proverbs, and make sure that students understand that even though a proverb can be thought of as a kind of "universal truth," it is an opinion and not a fact. *Part B:* Discuss the fact that most people have reasons for their opinions. Ask several volunteers to read an opinion on the page with which they agree and discuss why they agree with it. Then assign Part B for independent work, perhaps as homework.

Dear Dot

Dear Dot—

   My father is constantly criticizing me for the way I dress. He says that my dresses are too short and my jeans are too tight. And, of course, he thinks I use too much make-up. I have tried to explain to him about fashion but he just doesn't want to understand. He thinks I look "cheap." I tell him that's his opinion. My friends all dress the same way and their parents seem to accept it. What can I do?

Dress Code Blues

Discuss each of the questions in class. Then write your answers.

1. What does *criticize* mean? _____
_____

2. What is "constructive criticism"? _____
_____

3. Do you think the father is giving constructive criticism? Explain your answer._____
_____

4. Should a parent have the right to control what a teenager wears? Why or why not? _____
_____
_____

5. How can Dress Code Blues work out a compromise with her father? _____
_____
_____

Write About It

Now put yourself in Dot's place. Write a helpful answer to Dress Code Blues. Remember, you want to help solve the problem, not make fun of the writer or criticize her.

Dear Dress Code Blues—

_____
_____
_____
_____
_____
_____
_____
_____

Skill Objectives: Reading for details; building vocabulary; making judgments; expressing opinions in writing. Discuss the meanings of *criticize*, and elicit that its connotation is usually negative; help students contrast this with *constructive criticism*. Discuss each of the other questions, then have students write their answers. Suggest that they use these answers as a basis for their letters. You may wish to assign the letter-writing activity as homework.

68

He Used to Be Fat

Several years ago, Mr. Big was very fat. He went on a diet and lost 225 pounds! Now he is thin, happy, and healthy. He used to eat seven sandwiches for lunch, but he doesn't anymore. Now he eats a salad for lunch. He used to drink two bottles of cola with his lunch, but he doesn't anymore. Now he drinks one can of diet soda. He used to weigh 400 pounds, but he doesn't anymore. Now he weighs 175 pounds. He used to wear size 52 pants, but he doesn't anymore. Now he wears size 34. He used to stay home every Saturday night, but now he goes out on dates. He used to be unhappy and lonely, but he isn't anymore. Now he is happy and has a lot of friends.

Answer the questions below. Use complete sentences. The first one is done for you.

1. How did Mr. Big lose weight? _He went on a diet._

2. How much weight did he lose? _____

3. How many sandwiches did he use to eat? _____

4. Does he eat sandwiches for lunch now? _____

5. What does he eat for lunch now? _____

6. What did he use to drink with his lunch? _____

7. What does he drink now? _____

8. How much did he use to weigh? _____

9. What does he weigh now? _____

10. What size pants did he use to wear? _____

11. Does he wear that size now? _____

12. What size does he wear now? _____

13. What did he use to do on Saturday nights? _____

14. What does he do on Saturday nights now? _____

15. Is Mr. Big's life better or worse now? Why? _____

_____

Skill Objectives: Expressing past action with *used to*; reading for specific information; comparing and contrasting. Have students look at the illustrations and discuss them. Then have the paragraph between the illustrations read silently. Call attention to the repeated phrase *used to* and explain it as indicating continued action in the past that does not continue to the present. Do the first six items orally, being sure that students use *used to* in the third and sixth. Then assign the page as written work.

What Should You Do?

A. **Read the chart below, then write sentences with *should, ought to,* or *had better*.** The first two are done for you.

Problem	Solution
Lisa has the hiccups.	Drink some water.
Ed is very tired.	Get more rest.
Sam and Tom have stomachaches.	Lie down.
Mr. Ross drives very fast.	Slow down.
My car is making funny noises.	Take it to a mechanic.
You have a sore throat.	Gargle with salt and water.

1. *Lisa has the hiccups. She had better drink some water.*
2. *Ed is very tired. He ought to get more rest.*
3. _____
4. _____
5. _____
6. _____

B. **What do you think you should do in the following situations? Write your answers on the lines. Use complete sentences.**

1. You see a strange man entering a neighbor's house through a window. What should you do?

   _____

2. It is a very cold day and there's no heat in your apartment. What should you do?

   _____

3. Your friend, Eileen, smokes three packs of cigarettes a day. What should you do?

   _____

4. Your friend, George, has to take an important history test tomorrow morning. You are at a disco together now, and it's getting late. What should you do?

   _____

   _____

5. You and your friends are playing baseball in your backyard. You hit the ball through a neighbor's window. What should you do? Who should pay for the window? You? The team? Your neighbor?

   _____

   _____

Skill Objectives: Using modals *should, ought to, had better*; making judgments; writing solutions to problems. *Part A*: Elicit that all three modals have approximately the same meaning (obligation or logical necessity). Make sure students understand when to use the completer *to*. Call attention to the chart and the two "done for you" sentences; then have students write sentences for the other problems. *Part B*: Do all items orally, eliciting several responses for each, then assign as written work.

70

It's Possible!

A. Read the chart below, then fill in the missing possibilities. Your class will come up with many different answers.

Present Facts	Possibilities
Tom is sneezing.	a. He has an allergy. b. He has a cold.
Ed and Jim never eat candy.	a. They are on a diet. b. They don't like candy.
Laura is not in class today.	a. b.
It's 9:00 P.M. and the lights are out next door.	a. b.

B. Now write sentences about the situations on the chart. Use *may* or *might* plus the simple form of the verb. The first two are done for you.

1. _Tom might have an allergy or he might have a cold._
2. _Ed and Jim may be on a diet or they may not like candy._
3. _____
4. _____

C. Read the chart, then fill in the missing possibilities.

Facts About the Future	Possibilities
Callie is going to graduate soon.	a. She will get a job. b. She will go to college.
Tony is going to buy a new car.	a. He will buy a Ford. b. He will buy a Toyota.
Anna is going to college next year.	a. b.
I am going to take a vacation.	a. b.

D. Write sentences about the situations on the chart. Use *may* or *might* and the simple form of the verb. The first one is done for you.

1. _Callie might get a job or she might go to college._
2. _____
3. _____
4. _____

Skill Objectives: Expressing possibility with *might* or *may*; making inferences; drawing conclusions. *Part A:* Complete the chart orally, asking for as many responses as possible. *Part B:* Have students use the chart to write sentences, using the two completed items as models. Be sure students understand the changes in verb form between the chart and the response sentences. *Parts C and D:* Follow the same procedure as for Parts A and B. Point out that *might* and *may* can be used with statements about both present and future.

The Elephant Man

Dr. Frederick Treves first heard of the Elephant Man in 1886. Friends told him about a strange man who had been shown at the London circus. The man was so ugly and frightening that the police had come to close down the show. As a doctor, Treves became very interested in meeting the Elephant Man. He thought that he might be able to help him. He went to see the Elephant Man's manager, Tom Norman. Dr. Treves paid a special fee for the opportunity to see the Elephant Man alone.

Treves's friends had been right. The Elephant Man was extremely ugly. His head was huge. His skin was rough and wrinkled, like an elephant's. His back was bent and curved, and one arm was thick and useless. Tom Norman, the manager, explained, "His mother was frightened by an elephant when she was pregnant. The sad creature you see here is the startling result."

Dr. Treves knew that this was nonsense, but he said nothing. Instead, he asked if he could bring the Elephant Man to the hospital and examine him more completely. Norman agreed, and the doctor took the Elephant Man, with his face and body completely covered, to the hospital.

Dr. Treves had learned from Tom Norman that the Elephant Man's name was John Merrick, that he was 25 years old, and that he was British. In fact, the Elephant Man's name was Joseph, but due to this introduction, he became known to the world as John.

Dr. Treves hoped to find out more about his patient, but the Elephant Man refused to answer his questions. Treves concluded that the Elephant Man was an imbecile, totally unintelligent and unaware of his condition.

A few days after the medical examination, Dr. Treves presented the Elephant Man to the other doctors. They were shocked and amazed. Treves had hoped that together he and the other doctors might be able to find a cure for the patient. It took only a short time for the doctors to realize that there was nothing they could do for the poor man. Reluctantly, Dr. Treves sent the Elephant Man back to his manager.

Two years passed before Dr. Treves saw the Elephant Man again. During that time, the Elephant Man was sent on tour in Europe with a new manager. He met the same problems on the continent as he had encountered in England. The crowds were shocked and frightened by his ugliness, and demanded that the police close the show.

Merrick's new manager was even more cruel than Tom Norman. When he realized that the Elephant Man couldn't bring in any more money, he abandoned Merrick in Belgium. To make matters worse, the manager stole all of the Elephant Man's savings, leaving him with only enough money for a ticket home.

The trip back to London was a nightmare. Crowds of people followed the black-cloaked Elephant Man. They shouted at him and threw things at him. In London, he was attacked by a mob of men and boys. The police had to break up the crowd and rescue the Elephant Man. They were uncertain of what to do with the strange creature until he showed them a hospital card that Dr. Treves had given him two years earlier. Quickly, the police brought Merrick to Dr. Treves's hospital office.

Dr. Treves took the Elephant Man to a room on the top floor of the hospital. Day after day, he went to talk with Joseph Merrick, the Elephant Man. Soon the doctor realized that the sounds coming from Joseph's mouth were real words, not mumbled nonsense. This was no imbecile at all. The Elephant Man was an intelligent person and very aware of the harsh realities of his life. Dr. Treves was amazed that the young man had been able to survive in his world of cruelty for so long.

Dr. Treves wanted Joseph Merrick to communicate with other people. When Dr. Treves felt his patient's speech had improved enough to be understood, he invited a friend of his, a young, pretty widow, to come and visit Joseph. She had been told about the Elephant Man's appearance, but she was not afraid, and was quite willing to come.

When she got to Joesph's room, she entered, smiled, and shook his hand. Joseph Merrick began to cry loudly and uncontrollably. Dr. Treves hurried his friend out of the room, then rushed back to find

(Go on to the next page.)

Skill Objectives: Reading for main idea and details; building vocabulary. Ask students if they have heard of the Elephant Man. Some may have seen the movie about him; allow discussion of what they know about him. Then preview the following vocabulary: *wrinkled, nonsense, due to, refuse, imbecile, realize, encountered, nightmare, harsh, cruelty, kindness, jeer, humbly, suffocate, deformity.* When students seem comfortable with the words, have them read the story. Provide help if necessary.

out why Joseph had reacted so violently.

Merrick explained that no woman, except for the nurses, had ever smiled at him or treated him gently before. He was used to shouts of horror from strange women. For the first time in his life, he was experiencing the kindness of strangers, and it frightened him. Dr. Treves understood, but now more than ever, he wanted Joseph to meet and talk with other people.

Joseph Merrick soon learned to accept the kindness of others. He had become famous, without knowing it, when one of the hospital administrators wrote about him in the London Times. Soon society women, actresses, and even royalty came to visit him. They came not to stare and jeer, but to talk with this gentle man who loved life and literature.

Although he received many gifts and became quite famous, Joseph Merrick never grew conceited or bad-tempered. Every kindness and present amazed him, and he accepted it all humbly. After 27 years of cru-elty, his life had finally changed and had now become enjoyable and good.

One condition of Joseph's life could not and did not change. Joseph Merrick was still the Elephant Man. There was no cure for the disease that was attacking his body. He was bent and misshapen and unable to move about easily or sleep normally.

On April 11, 1890, about two years after his admittance to the London Hospital, Joseph Merrick died. Dr. Treves theorized that Joseph had been trying out a new sleeping position when his head slipped back too far, and the weight of it caused him to suffocate. Life had ended as cruelly as it had begun.

After his patient's death, Dr. Treves remarked that while Joseph Merrick was perhaps the ugliest man he had ever seen, he was also the most beautiful, in character and in spirit. That is a fitting tribute to Joseph Merrick, the Elephant Man, a man whose gentle and loving nature was able to shine through his physical deformity.

A. Read each statement below and decide if it is a fact or an opinion. Circle F if it is a fact. Circle O if it is an opinion.

F   O   1. Joseph Merrick had been shown in a circus.

F   O   2. Joseph Merrick was a British citizen.

F   O   3. Joseph Merrick was too ugly to show to people.

F   O   4. The police were unfair to close down the show.

F   O   5. An elephant caused Joseph Merrick's disease.

F   O   6. Joseph Merrick was an imbecile.

F   O   7. Joseph Merrick was unaware of his condition.

F   O   8. Joseph Merrick was known to the world as John.

F   O   9. The doctors were unable to cure Joseph Merrick.

F   O   10. The crowds on the continent were crueler than the ones in England.

F   O   11. The young widow was not afraid of Joseph Merrick.

F   O   12. It is difficult to accept the kindness of others.

F   O   13. Joseph Merrick was the ugliest man in history.

F   O   14. Joseph Merrick died on April 11, 1890.

B. People say that beauty is in the eye of the beholder. What do you think makes a person beautiful? Is it only physical beauty, or is there an inner beauty too? **On your paper, write a paragraph about what you think makes a person beautiful. Share your paragraph with the class. You will see there are many different definitions of beauty.**

Skill Objectives: Distinguishing between fact and opinion; expressing opinions in writing; interpreting proverbs. *Part A:* Review the difference between fact and opinion and true/false exercises, then assign the items. When students have finished, ask for other facts in the story, and discuss the characters. *Part B:* Discuss current and past ideas of beauty, and the ideas of beauty in different cultures. Read and talk about the topic for Part B. You may wish to assign the paragraph writing as homework.

73

I'd Rather Stay Home

> *Would rather* means "to prefer." Read the example below.
> —Would you rather go to a movie or watch TV tonight?
> —I'd (I would) rather stay home and watch TV.

A. Answer the questions. Tell what you would rather do. The first one is done for you.

1. Would you rather live in the country or in the city?
   I'd rather live in the city.

2. Would you rather learn French or Chinese?
   _____

3. Would you rather be a doctor or a lawyer?
   _____

4. Would you rather play the piano or the guitar?
   _____

5. Would you rather drive a Ford or a Toyota?
   _____

6. Would you rather be the oldest or the youngest in a family?
   _____

7. Would you rather wash the dishes or vacuum the living room?
   _____

8. Would you rather go to a big party or go out with a few friends?
   _____

B. What would these people rather do? Look at the picture, then answer the question. The first one is done for you.

1. Susan: wear jeans/a dress
   Susan would rather wear jeans than a dress.

2. Bob: listen to records/clean his room
   _____

3. We: drink coffee/orange juice
   _____

4. Ken and Barb: play tennis/soccer
   _____

5. My mother: live in an apartment/a house
   _____

6. They: stay in a hotel/go camping
   _____

Skill Objective: Expressing preference with *would rather*. Elicit that the use of *would rather* implies a stated or unstated alternate to the action with which it is used. Be sure students understand that *would rather* does not take the completer *to;* such small details are important in written and oral communication, and errors are noticeable to native speakers. *Part A:* Read and discuss the instructions, then assign as written work. *Part B:* Tell students to use the illustrations as clues for their answers.

Take It With a Grain of Salt

Slang expressions don't mean what they seem to say. They have special meanings that must be learned. **Try to match the slang expressions in Column A to their meanings in Column B. The dictionary explains many of these expressions. Use the dictionary if you need help.** The first item is done for you.

1. Have you buried the hatchet? _s_

2. Kill two birds with one stone. ____

3. It's raining cats and dogs! ____

4. You let the cat out of the bag. ____

5. Did you foot the bill? ____

6. Did you learn it by heart? ____

7. You gave them the cold shoulder. ____

8. Did you get cold feet? ____

9. We don't see eye to eye. ____

10. We were shooting the breeze. ____

11. Hold your horses! ____

12. No use crying over spilt milk. ____

13. You have to face the music. ____

14. Are you down in the dumps? ____

15. Are you moonlighting? ____

16. Are you going Dutch? ____

17. You hit the nail on the head. ____

18. Have you tied the knot? ____

19. You passed with flying colors! ____

20. You didn't cut the mustard. ____

21. Don't knock it! ____

22. You pulled a fast one. ____

23. You swallowed it hook, line, and sinker. ____

24. You have bats in your belfry. ____

25. Let's hit the hay. ____

a. Did you get married?
b. Did you pay for everybody?
c. You must confront the problem.
d. Get both things done at the same time.
e. We don't agree.
f. Don't criticize or make fun of it.
g. Are you paying your own way? (on a date)
h. That's exactly right.
i. We were just talking.
j. You didn't do well enough.
k. You were unfriendly to them.
l. Don't worry about something that's already been done.
m. It's raining very hard.
n. You tricked somebody.
o. Do you have a second job?
p. You got a very good grade.
q. Did you memorize it?
r. Did you get scared and decide not to do it?
s. Have you made peace?
t. You're crazy!
u. You told the secret.
v. Wait a minute!
w. Let's go to bed.
x. Are you depressed?
y. You believed it completely.

Skill Objective: Interpreting figurative language. Read (or have a student read) the introductory paragraph and discuss it with the class; make sure students understand the concept of slang expressions; ask volunteers for some from their native languages. If practical, do the page as a group activity; this way the collective knowledge of the group is shared (and an opportunity is provided for free communication). If some phrases stump the class, discuss use of the process of elimination and "educated guessing."

75

Reading the Newspaper: Just for Fun

Most newspapers print a daily horoscope. A horoscope is a "just for fun" feature. It tells your fortune according to your birthdate. **Read the horoscope predictions below, then answer the questions.**

MAR 21–APR 19 · ARIES

There might be problems at work today. Your boss may be angry with you. Keep smiling, and don't lose your temper!

APR 20–MAY 20 · TAURUS

You would rather stay home tonight, but this is a good time for you to meet people. Forget about your problems. Go out and socialize!

MAY 21–JUN 21 · GEMINI

You may begin the week feeling uncertain, but by Saturday you will see that everything is going quite well. Don't get discouraged.

JUN 22–JUL 22 · CANCER

Good luck is coming your way. Travel will be especially beneficial for you this month. Hop on a train or plane as soon as possible.

JUL 23–AUG 22 · LEO

You'd better slow down. You have been pushing yourself too hard over the past weeks. Slow down and rest up.

AUG 23–SEP 22 · VIRGO

Watch out for a trouble maker. You might believe some tales that are not true. Avoid strangers this week.

SEP 23–OCT 23 · LIBRA

You may feel left out this week. Don't worry; your friends and family care about you. Share your feelings with them.

OCT 24–NOV 21 · SCORPIO

You must pay back old debts this week. It might be dangerous to keep certain "friends" waiting.

NOV 22–DEC 21 · SAGITTARIUS

Help people around you who seem confused or upset. You may receive a great reward for your kindness.

DEC 22–JAN 19 · CAPRICORN

You had better find out just what your loved ones expect from you. You may be approaching a home situation incorrectly.

JAN 20–FEB 18 · AQUARIUS

You ought to try getting in touch with some old friends. They may be able to help you solve a problem.

FEB 19–MAR 20 · PISCES

Be careful with your hard-earned money. A "friend" may be more interested in your wallet than in you.

Skill Objectives: Reading for main ideas and details; understanding modals. Have students read the complete page, then reread it, underlining all the words that show possibility or future time. Extension: Discuss horoscopes and the ancient belief that the position of the stars affects human life. Point out that newspaper horoscopes are general enough so that they could apply to just about any situation. Students might bring in several different newspaper horoscopes for the same day and compare them.

76

A. 1. Who may be helpful to Aquarius this week? _____

2. How does Taurus feel today? _____

3. What does the horoscope promise Cancer? _____

4. Why may Leo be headed for trouble? _____

5. Who might be dangerous to Scorpio? _____

6. Why should Pisces be suspicious of a friend? _____

7. Where can Aries expect problems? _____

8. How will Gemini feel at the end of the week? _____

9. Why should Virgo be alert to trouble makers? _____

10. Where does the horoscope say Capricorn may be having trouble? _____

11. How does Libra feel? _____

12. What may happen if Sagittarius is helpful to others? _____

_____

B. Write down the birthdays of four friends or family members. Look up each person's sign on the horoscope, then write one sentence telling the person what he or she should or should not do.

Name	Birthday	Sign	Advice

C. The word game below is a format found in many newspapers. The riddle next to the picture is a pun. **To solve the puzzle, read the five sentences and fill in the missing words. Then copy the circled letters onto the lines under the riddle, matching the numbers.**

Question: What happened in Alaska to the daring young man on the flying trapeze?

Answer:

He __ __ __   __ __ __ __   __ __ __ __
   3 2 10   6 4 1 5   8 7 11 9

1. The lion represents this horoscope sign.

    __ __ __
    1 2

2. All that glitters is not . . .

    __ __ __
    3 4 5

3. George Washington was born under this sign.

    __ __ __ __ __
     6 7

4. If the shoe . . ., wear it!

    __ __ __
    8 9

5. . . . it easy!

    __ __ __
    10 11

Skill Objectives: Using modals to answer questions; solving a puzzle; completing a chart. *Part A:* Do the questions orally; ask for answers in complete sentence form and be sure students use the modals from the questions in their answers; then have them write short answers for the questions. *Part B:* Assign for independent work. *Part C:* Review the instructions, and explain what a pun is; then have students work in pairs to complete the puzzle. (The answer is on page 125.)

77

Find the Error (1)

There is a grammatical error in one of the underlined words or phrases in each sentence below. Find the error and circle it. Then correct the error in the blank under the sentence. The first one is done for you.

1. <u>Both</u> California and New York <u>have</u> big populations, but California is (more large) than New York <u>in area</u>.

   larger

2. Spanish <u>speak</u> in Argentina, but <u>Portuguese</u> is the <u>language of Brazil</u>.

   _____

3. If you <u>want</u> my <u>advice</u>, you <u>should better</u> study, or <u>you'll</u> never pass the test tomorrow.

   _____

4. <u>It's</u> difficult to <u>believe</u>, but I <u>have been studied</u> Chinese for the <u>past two years</u>.

   _____

5. After <u>Nancy took</u> a shower, combed <u>her</u> hair, and <u>made</u> her lunch, she <u>was going</u> to school.

   _____

6. The children <u>were</u> <u>extreme anxious</u> to know who the <u>winner was</u>.

   _____

7. Mary was <u>surprised</u> that the books <u>costed</u> $40.00. She expected <u>them</u> to be <u>much cheaper</u>.

   _____

8. I think <u>you'll</u> like the car I <u>just bought</u>; <u>it's</u> the same color <u>to</u> Mark's.

   _____

9. Your cousin is <u>old enough</u> to vote <u>in</u> the <u>upcoming</u> election, <u>doesn't he</u>?

   _____

10. I know <u>from experience</u> that <u>the</u> grass will not grow in this yard if you <u>didn't water</u> it <u>frequently</u>.

    _____

11. John <u>tripped</u> and <u>broke his</u> arm while he <u>was crossed</u> the street.

    _____

12. You <u>must to be</u> at <u>least</u> 16 years old to <u>apply</u> for a license <u>in this state</u>.

    _____

13. When <u>the girls and I</u> arrived <u>at</u> the theater, <u>the</u> movie <u>had already been started</u>.

    _____

14. I <u>was used</u> to spend <u>a lot of</u> time <u>playing pool</u>, but now I have a full time job, and that keeps me <u>pretty busy</u>.

    _____

15. <u>Most of the people</u> in <u>this</u> room <u>speak</u> several languages <u>and I do so</u>.

    _____

Dear Dot

Dear Dot—

I will be graduating in June and am very confused about my future. I have been accepted at college and I want to go, but on the other hand I want to make some money and get into "the real world." I studied typing and accounting in school, so I know I could get a job that pays fairly well. Should I get a job or should I continue with school? I'm not sure what I want to do at college, so I am leaning much more towards work. Please advise.

Graduate-to-be

Discuss each of the questions in class. Then write your answers.

1. What does "the real world" mean? _____

_____

2. What are the advantages of going to college? _____

_____

3. What are the advantages of going to work? _____

_____

4. What compromise solution can you suggest to Graduate-to-be? _____

_____

5. Do you think you will face the same problem when you finish high school? What decision do you think you will make? Why? _____

_____

Write About It

Now put yourself in Dot's place. Write a helpful answer to Graduate-to-be. Remember, you want to help solve the problem, not make fun of the writer or criticize.

Dear Graduate-to-be—

_____

_____

_____

_____

_____

_____

_____

_____

Skill Objectives: Interpreting figurative language; making judgments; drawing conclusions; expressing opinions in writing.
Have students read the letter. Discuss each question in class. Be sure students can support their opinions. This letter raises questions that are very important to students; allow ample time for the discussion. After students have written their answers to the questions, they can incorporate them in their letters.

Gerunds: When Verbs Become Nouns

A gerund is a noun made out of a verb—a *verbal noun.* Gerunds are used as nouns, but they look exactly like present participles. Like present participles, they end in *-ing.* Like a noun, a gerund can be the subject of a sentence. It can also be used after a verb as the object of a sentence. Gerunds can be used with only certain verbs, however. With other verbs, it is necessary to use an infinitive instead of a gerund. Look at the two examples:

Jasmine avoids *exercising.*   (gerund)
Jasmine refuses *to exercise.*   (infinitive)

Look at the three boxes. The first box shows verbs that can be followed by a gerund. The second shows verbs that can be followed by either a gerund or an infinitive. The third shows verbs that can be followed only by an infinitive.

Gerund Only		Gerund or Infinitive		Infinitive Only	
admit	enjoy	begin	love	afford	hope
appreciate	finish	cease	neglect	agree	learn
avoid	mind	continue	prefer	choose	plan
consider	practice	hate	start	decide	refuse
deny	stop	like	try	forget	want

Complete the sentences using a gerund or an infinitive form of the verb in parentheses. The first one is done for you.

1. Lauri enjoys ____*playing*____ (play) the violin.

2. Ronald started _____ (take) piano lessons two months ago.

3. Don't forget _____ (do) your homework.

4. I don't mind _____ (do) the laundry.

5. Do you want _____ (have) lunch with me today?

6. Tom and Maria like _____ (dance).

7. I'm glad that I've finally finished _____ (paint) the kitchen.

8. Where did you learn _____ (play) the guitar so well?

9. My mother hopes _____ (return) to her job soon.

10. Bill continued _____ (talk) even though Mrs. Jones asked him to stop.

11. Juan practices _____ (speak) English every day.

12. I can't afford _____ (buy) a Mercedes.

13. My sister prefers _____ (read) love stories instead of mysteries.

14. Paula hates _____ (wash) the dishes.

15. Will you consider _____ (take) this job?

16. I'd love _____ (go) with you if I could spare the time.

17. Vuong is planning _____ (take) a trip to San Francisco this spring.

18. You'll have to stop _____ (make) so much noise!

19. Meredith will begin _____ (work) in her new office next week.

20. Kate has chosen _____ (continue) her education after all.

Skill Objective: Choosing between gerunds and infinitives. Read the introductory paragraphs with the class, and make sure that students understand the difference between the two structures. Have students look at the three boxes, and give some examples: *I enjoy reading; I hate exercising* or *I hate to exercise; I hope to read that book.* Emphasize the importance of accurate usage in written and oral English. Then assign the items for written work.

Gerunds and Prepositions

A gerund preceded by a preposition is a *gerund phrase.* Look at the example:

Binh is interested *in going* to the pool today.

In the example, *in going* is a gerund phrase.

A. Complete the gerund phrase in each of the following sentences by filling the blank with a gerund that makes sense in the sentence. The first one is done for you.

1. Thank you for _____*coming*_____ to my party.

2. Always wash your hands before _____ dinner.

3. I am interested in _____ to Disneyland.

4. Always look both ways before _____ the street.

5. Susanna is tired of _____ English.

6. Mr. Jones has been working at the bank for 30 years. Now he is 64 years old and is thinking about _____.

7. You should always read the directions on the container before _____ any medicine.

8. Do you have a recipe for _____ chocolate cake?

9. Before _____ the room, you should turn off all the lights.

10. Maria is thinking of _____ to Harvard University.

B. Find a gerund that makes sense for each of the blanks, and write it in the blank.

Lari is a musician. She enjoys _____ many musical instruments. Lari started _____ the violin two years ago, but she began _____ piano lessons ten years ago when she was a little girl. She is also interested in _____ how to play the flute. _____ the piano and the violin every day takes a lot of time, however, so she thinks she'll wait another year before _____ flute lessons.

Lari likes _____ in New York City because she can go to lots of concerts. She prefers _____ to classical music, but she also enjoys _____ to jazz.

When Lari gets tired of _____ the violin and the piano, she likes _____ in the Palisades Interstate Park across the Hudson River from New York. Lately, Lari has been thinking about _____ to the Juilliard School of Music when she finishes high school.

C. On your paper write the same three paragraphs about Lari, substituting infinitives for gerunds wherever you can.

Skill Objectives: Using gerunds after prepositions; using gerunds and infinitives to complete sentences. Read the introductory material; be sure students understand what is meant by the term *gerund phrase.* Part A: Do the first three items orally; be sure students choose gerunds that make logical sense in the sentences; then assign as written work. Part B: Assign as written work, then have several students give their choices for the blanks. Part C: After this has been completed, go over it with the class.

81

Adjectives Ending in -*ed* and -*ing*

> Some adjectives have two different forms. Look at the following examples:
> **confused – confusing   interested – interesting   excited – exciting**
>
> Adjectives ending in -*ing* usually express a person's opinion about something:
> **The speech was confusing.   That subject is interesting.   Your idea is exciting.**
>
> Adjectives ending in -*ed* usually express an emotion, how someone feels:
> **I am very confused.   I am interested in that subject.   He was excited by my idea.**

A. Circle the correct form of the adjective in each sentence. The first one is done for you.

1. We were (surprised / surprising) when the rain started.

2. That movie was the most (amazed / amazing) film I've ever seen.

3. The news was (shocked / shocking).

4. The children were (stunned / stunning) when they found out.

5. That film was (frightened / frightening).

6. The accident was (horrified / horrifying) to see.

7. Emily was (embarrassed / embarrassing) when she spilled coffee on her blouse.

8. Skiing is an (excited / exciting) sport.

9. My mother was (pleased / pleasing) with her gift.

10. That program was the most (bored / boring) one I have ever seen.

11. Science is a (fascinated / fascinating) subject.

12. This book is the most (interested / interesting) one I have read in a long time.

13. The students were (relieved / relieving) when the test was canceled.

14. John's report was very (confused / confusing); I didn't understand it at all.

15. The puppies were (terrified / terrifying) by the noise of the fireworks.

16. My sister felt (satisfied / satisfying) with her grades.

17. She is the most (bored / boring) teacher in school. I'm always (bored / boring) in her class.

18. Mr. Collins has a (surprised / surprising) number of books about World War II.

19. They have never been (interested / interesting) in learning about other cultures.

20. Of course we were very (disappointed / disappointing) to lose last night's game.

B. Now write a sentence on your paper for each of the following words. Make sure you use them as adjectives. Do not copy any of the sentences in Part A.

thrilled	astonished	bored	excited	tired
thrilling	astonishing	boring	exciting	tiring

Skill Objectives: Using -*ed*/-*ing* adjectives correctly; expanding vocabulary; differentiating between two forms of the same word. Explain that -*ed* and -*ing* words can be used as adjectives as well as verbs. Review the boxed explanation at the top of the page and discuss the differences in meaning between the -*ed* and -*ing* forms of the same word. Then assign Part A for independent work. *Part B:* You may wish to have students write their sentences as homework.

What's the Sport?

Read the sentences at the left and decide which sport each one is telling about. Write the letter of that sport in the blank. Each sentence has one or more vocabulary clues to help you identify the sport. The first one is done for you.

_k_ 1. Don't worry. You can buy new laces at the rink.

___ 2. Frank likes to do three miles a day. It usually takes him about 25 minutes.

___ 3. The four friends picked up their racquets and went to the courts.

___ 4. A sudden gust of wind caught the spinnaker and almost overturned the small boat.

___ 5. The puck flew off the ice and into the stands.

___ 6. I did 20 laps in the pool this morning.

___ 7. Only the goalie can touch the ball with the hands.

___ 8. Pull your bow back and aim for the dot right in the middle of the target.

___ 9. Gerri dribbled quickly as she ran down the court.

___ 10. After Ben knocked down all the pins, he won the match.

___ 11. Back and forth the ball bounced on the table until finally Jane missed her shot and Rosie scored a point.

___ 12. Mario ran down the track, leaned on his stick, and flew over the bar.

___ 13. After Bruno got Wild Bill in a headlock, he threw him down on the mat, and the referee counted him out.

___ 14. The white ball slammed into the 15 colored ones, and it was the 6 ball in the corner pocket and the 12 on the side.

___ 15. After putting the bait on the line, you've got to sit in the boat and wait for a bite.

___ 16. The players stood in a huddle and listened as the quarterback explained what to do.

___ 17. All the fans had their eyes on the mound, waiting to see what the nervous pitcher would do.

___ 18. Betty stood at the top of the mountain. She dug her poles into the snow and pushed herself out and down.

___ 19. Rick landed a quick right, a stinging left, and a couple of jabs, and his opponent was down, knocked out in the fourth round.

___ 20. Becky swung her driver, and the little white ball sailed in the air and landed on the green.

a. bowling

b. basketball

c. hockey

d. soccer

e. wrestling

f. pole-vaulting

g. tennis

h. baseball

i. golf

j. fishing

k. skating

l. boxing

m. swimming

n. sailing

o. football

p. table tennis

q. archery

r. skiing

s. pool

t. jogging

Skill Objectives: Classifying; using context clues; making inferences; interpreting figurative language. Read the directions at the top of the page. Ask students to underline the words in each example that are the context clues (e.g. *rink* in item1). Allow time for students to read through both columns before attempting the matching exercise. If possible, do the page as a group activity to let students share their collective knowledge and find trickier answers by the process of elimination.

83

You've Got a Problem

Solve the following problems. Use the bottom of the page to figure on if you need to. The first problem is done for you.

Your Answer

1. The Bullets have won half of their games this season. They have played 90 games so far. How many have they won?

   45

2. To figure a batting average, divide the number of hits by the number of times a person has attempted to hit. Carry your division out to three decimal places. What is the batting average of a person who has hit

   12 times in 60 attempts? _____

   15 times in 60 attempts? _____

   18 times in 59 attempts? _____

   33 times in 102 attempts? _____

3. If 579 fans paid $1.50 each to attend last week's basketball game at Dover Falls High School, how much money did the school take in that night? _____

4. If one of the members of the swim team can swim 75 yards in one minute, how far can she swim in a quarter of an hour? _____

5. Jules Lemmon, a professional football player, earned $30,000 in his first year as a pro. He earned $45,000 in his second year, $54,000 in his third, and $65,000 in his fourth year. In his fifth and final year as a player, Jules earned $72,000. What was his average salary for the five years that he was a professional player? _____

6. While practicing for a race, a race car driver drove steadily at 140 m.p.h. for thirty minutes. How far did he drive in that time? _____

7. Molly ran the hundred-yard dash in 17.26 seconds. Carmen ran it in 16.37 seconds. What was the difference in their times? _____

8. A hockey player scores a point for each goal he makes. The player also scores a point for helping another player to make a goal (an assist). How many points does each of the following players have if they have made:

   35 goals and 39 assists? _____

   49 goals and 47 assists? _____

   46 goals and 61 assists? _____

   43 goals and 38 assists? _____

Skill Objective: Solving mathematical word problems. Ask students to read quickly through the problems and underline or circle any terms that are unfamiliar; explain these terms. Allow time for students to do the problems, then have volunteers put the math work on the board and let individual students explain their problem-solving methods. (Answers are on page 125.)

Adjective Form or Noun Form?

> Many words have similar adjective and noun forms. Look at the following examples:
> **different – difference   important – importance   impatient – impatience**
>
> Use the adjective form to tell which or what kind. Use adjectives before nouns or after forms of *to be.*
> See the sentences below:
> **We have different opinions about Joe.   Karen and I are very different.**
>
> Use the noun form to express the quality that someone or something has:
> **Identical twins have few physical differences.   Silence is required in the library.**

A. **Circle the correct form in each sentence. (The adjective form is always first and the noun form is second.)** The first one is done for you.

1. It is very (**important**/ importance) to be on time.

2. Jose has only one (absent / absence) from school.

3. The man maintained his (innocent / innocence) throughout the trial.

4. (Adolescent / Adolescence) is a difficult time of life.

5. You have to be very (patient / patience) to teach kindergarten students.

6. Many college students are (dependent / dependence) on the government for tuition money.

7. The view of the mountains was (magnificent / magnificence).

8. The (ignorant / ignorance) of the people was shocking.

9. If you look in the (distant / distance) you can see the sea.

10. The children were (confident / confidence) of winning.

11. The United States is (tolerant / tolerance) of all religions.

12. You mustn't be (negligent / negligence) about dental care.

13. Her (present / presence) at the party made it a success.

14. The boss fired the two (incompetent / incompetence) workers.

15. The United States declared its (independent / independence) from England in 1776.

16. The boy was (silent / silence) when the principal questioned him.

17. I'm (confident / confidence) that I'll do well on the test.

18. Her rudeness and (insolent / insolence) upset all of us.

19. The table was loaded with an (abundant / abundance) of food.

20. The President assured us he would be (present / presence) at the ceremony.

B. **Now write a sentence on your paper for each of the following words. Do not copy any of the sentences in Part A. Use a dictionary if you need to.**

dependent	important	reluctant	affluent	different
dependence	importance	reluctance	affluence	difference

Skill Objectives: Choosing between adjectives and nouns; building vocabulary; internalizing grammar rules. Review the boxed explanation of adjectives and nouns at the top of the page. Make sure students understand the concept of nouns, pronouns, and adjectives. Do a few examples as a class, then assign students independent time to complete the page on their own. Review the page together, with students taking turns reading the complete sentences aloud and explaining their choices.

Reading the Newspaper:
The Sports Pages

The sports pages of the newspaper bring together a variety of stories on many different sports. In the same issue of a newspaper you are likely to find stories on baseball, football, basketball, hockey, golf, horse racing, track and field, swimming, and any other sport that is played in the newspaper's area. There are stories about school sports, college sports, and professional sports. Often there are interviews with players or managers. And there are reports of games, races, or other contests that have just taken place.

Sports writing is *idiomatic.* It is full of colorful images and slang expressions. Some people say that sports language is a language all its own.

Read the following story from the sports pages. Then answer the questions.

DYNAMO WIN STREAK KEEPS ON CHARGING AS SPRINGERS FALL 8–2

Sparks flew from the Dynamos' energized bats and the inspired hurling of Sunny Tatum yesterday when the victory-minded locals downed the Springfield Springers at Jackson Stadium.

The game was a losing battle for the hardworking but outclassed Springers as Tony Suarez gave up hit after hit to the fearless foursome, the first four batters in the Dynamo starting lineup.

Chuck Barres started the fireworks when he doubled on Suarez's first pitch. Jim Eagle singled, then Junior Fitch hit a long drive to center field that brought in Barres. With the score at 1–0, Big Boy Gibson swatted the horsehide pellet up, up, and away, where it's probably still in orbit. The inning ended with the Dynamos ahead by an impressive 5–0.

With Shorty Weiss replacing Suarez, the game settled down to a pitchers' contest. Tatum was at his artful best as he hurled sliders and curves past the Springer batters. So well did he propel the ball that not one Springer in the first six innings got a chance to run the 90 feet that starts a batter on his path to glory.

Weiss, probably the best first year pitcher in any bullpen, performed nearly as well, giving up only one hit in the fourth inning and two more in the sixth, including another homer for Gibson. At this point Springer manager Ralph Norton replaced Weiss with relief pitcher Max Koralski. Madman Max kept the Dynamos hitless for the next two innings, while Art Jones and Bill Fry managed to score two runs against Tatum.

The Dynamo express came to life again in the ninth when Mighty Mike Malone, who moonlights as the Aftershave King on TV commercials, singled and was followed by center fielder Carl Zuccone, who sent the ball out of the park for his first homer of the season.

The Springers' best wasn't good enough, and Tatum kept them hitless through the last half of the ninth for a fifth-in-a-row Dynamo victory of 8–2. Joe Balch, veteran Dynamo fan, had one word for the game: "Superb!" he said. He should know. This is Joe's sixty-eighth Dynamo season.

A. Answer these questions about the story.

1. What sport is being described in the story? _____

2. What position does Tony Suarez play on which team? _____
_____

3. What phrase tells you that the Dynamos were hitting well? _____
_____

4. What word does the writer use for *throwing*? _____
_____

5. What does the writer mean by "the 90 feet that starts a batter on his path to glory"?
_____
_____

(Go on to the next page.)

Skill Objectives: Reading comprehension; understanding figurative language; understanding words through context. Read and discuss the introductory paragraphs. Emphasize and clarify the idea of idiomatic expressions. Have students read the story silently and underline or circle idiomatic expressions, figurative language, and specialized sports terms (*bullpen, singled, homer, etc.*) Extension: Lead a discussion on why sports have such appeal. What are the major sports in students' native countries? Why?

6. What phrase does the writer use to describe Carl Zuccone's home run? _____
_____
_____

7. What is Max Koralski's nickname? _____
_____

8. What phrase says that the Dynamos scored no runs in the 7th and 8th innings? _____
_____

9. What is a bullpen? _____
_____

10. Why is Joe Balch described as a "veteran fan"? What does the word *veteran* mean
in this phrase? _____
_____

B. Write a summary of the story using ordinary English. Use more paper if you need to.

_____
_____
_____
_____
_____
_____
_____
_____
_____
_____
_____
_____
_____
_____
_____
_____
_____

C. Bring in a sports story from your local newspaper. Write questions about it similar to those in section A, and have a partner answer them. With your partner, make a brief dictionary of some of the colorful or idiomatic expressions in the story, giving their meaning in ordinary English.

D. Go to a sports contest or game and write a description of it. Try to use colorful language to make the game "come alive" in the reader's mind. Test your readers after they have read your story to see how well they have understood what actually happened at the game or contest.

Skill Objectives: Drawing conclusions; locating specific information; using context clues. *Part A:* Assign the questions as independent work, then discuss answers with the class. *Part B:* You may wish to post stories and questions on the bulletin board. Ask students for new expressions (and their meanings) that they found in their stories. *Part C:* Have each story read by several students; then discuss some of the common problems students faced in writing their stories—and their solutions.

87

Your Choice of Words

Use the context of sentences to find the right words to complete them.

Each sentence contains a pair of blanks. Complete each sentence with the appropriate set of words. Use a dictionary if you need to. The first one is done for you.

1. I could _____barely_____ hear the announcer so I _____turned up_____ the volume on the television set.
   - a. quietly/opened
   - c. hugely/turned off
   - b. barely/turned up
   - d. nervously/answered

2. When people work in _____ conditions, it's not unusual for _____ to develop.
   - a. handsome/rivalries
   - c. crowded/tensions
   - b. perfect/imperfections
   - d. dark/delight

3. The _____ who performed that operation was recently _____ as the top doctor in the tri-state region.
   - a. surgeon/honored
   - c. candidate/elected
   - b. nurse/fired
   - d. veteran/awarded

4. _____ people have been injured at this intersection that a new traffic light will be _____ as soon as possible.
   - a. Too many/ignored
   - c. So many/installed
   - b. Such/destroyed
   - d. How many/broken

5. The farmers are expecting a below-normal _____ due to the _____ rainfall this year.
   - a. harvest/sparse
   - c. farm/disorganized
   - b. animal/abundant
   - d. production/wet

6. There was a _____ feeling at the factory after the news of the closing was _____ .
   - a. cheery/described
   - c. consistent/rejected
   - b. melancholy/announced
   - d. peculiar/translated

7. _____ several months of hard work, Jacob's entry in the science fair did not win any of the _____ prizes.
   - a. For/final
   - c. Despite/major
   - b. Because of/influential
   - d. Just as/important

8. The jury listened _____ while the defense lawyer presented his _____ remarks.
   - a. haphazardly/unkind
   - c. thoroughly/irrelevant
   - b. attentively/opening
   - d. friendly/remarkable

9. Gardening is a relaxing _____ for Mrs. Sanchez who has a stressful job as a stockbroker in a _____ Wall Street company.
   - a. job/corporate
   - c. portrait/growing
   - b. flowers/leading
   - d. hobby/large

Skill Objectives: Understanding vocabulary in context; preparing for standardized tests. Explain to students that this type of exercise is similar to those found on some standardized tests. Explain that they must read each sentence completely—both the words before and those after the blanks—in order to get an idea of what the sentence is saying and thus know which pair of words to pick to go in the blanks. Warn students that they must use both words in a single pair—they cannot use one word from one pair and another from a second pair. Discuss the first item and be sure students understand why pair b was chosen. Then assign the page for independent work.

Dear Dot

Dear Dot—

Vacation is coming, and I dread it. Everyone starts playing sports, and I am no good at any of them. I have to stay at home or just watch from the sidelines. I would love to play, but I am a first-class klutz, and I never can seem to do the right thing when I am playing any sport. In school when I have to play I am always the last one picked for any team. Is there anything I can do to improve my sports ability?

Loser

Discuss each of the questions in class. Then write your answers.

1. What is a *klutz*? _____
   _____

2. How does a person become good at anything? _____
   _____
   _____

3. What is confidence? Is confidence important in sports? _____
   _____
   _____

4. How can Loser change? _____
   _____
   _____

Write About It

Now put yourself in Dot's place. Write a helpful answer to Loser. Remember, you want to help solve the problem, not make fun of the writer or criticize.

Dear Loser—

_____
_____
_____
_____
_____
_____
_____
_____
_____

Skill Objectives: Reading for main idea; understanding figurative language; making judgments; expressing opinions in writing.
Have students read the letter. Review the questions orally, and encourage as much dialogue as possible; be sure students support their opinions. Then have students write answers to the questions. Suggest they use these answers as the basis for their letters. You may wish to assign the letter-writing activity as homework.

Taxes and Pay Slips

A. Everyone who earns more than a small amount of money has to pay a federal income tax. Many states also have a state income tax. People in these states have to pay both a federal and a state income tax.

Federal Income Tax. The federal income tax is a *graduated tax.* This means that people who make a lot of money pay taxes at a higher rate than people who make less money. Federal taxes pay for the military, space programs, interstate highways, and many other programs.

State Income Tax. Some states have a graduated tax, others have a flat percentage rate which can vary from 3% to 17% depending on the state. State tax money goes to state roads, welfare, and other state programs. Does your state have a state income tax? Is it a graduated tax or a fixed percentage?

Write *True* or *False* after each sentence below.

1. Everyone who earns more than a small amount of money has to pay a federal income tax. _____

2. Everyone who has a job in the U.S. has to pay state income tax. _____

3. A person who makes $30,000 a year pays the same federal income tax as a person who makes $10,000 a year. _____

4. State taxes pay for the army, navy, and air force. _____

B. Income tax, Social Security, and health insurance payments are often taken out of your salary before you receive your money. A pay slip, or the stub of your paycheck explains what money is taken out of your pay.

Statement of Earnings and Deductions
Detach and Retain

Period Ending ___Aug. 15___

Name ___Juan Perez___

			$	
$18.00/hr.	Regular Hours	40	720	00
$27.00/hr.	Overtime Hours	9	243	00
Total Earnings			963	00
F.I.C.A. (Social Security)	73	66		
Fed. Income Tax	165	00		
State Income Tax	50	84		
Health Insurance	96	—		
Total Deductions			385	50
Net Earnings			577	50

Juan Perez is an electrician and is paid every week. He has a full time job and often works overtime. **Read his pay slip and complete these sentences.**

1. Juan makes _____ an hour.

2. Overtime work pays _____ an hour.

3. His total earnings, before anything was deducted, were _____.

4. His net, or take-home, pay was

    _____.

5. He paid _____ in federal income tax.

6. He paid _____ in state income tax.

7. He paid _____ for Social Security and _____ for health insurance.

8. His total deductions were

    _____.

Skill Objectives: Reading for details; understanding taxes; getting information from forms. *Part A:* Read (or have students read) the first three paragraphs and discuss them. Be sure students understand the difference between a graduated and a flat-rate tax. Discuss which kind your state has. Tell students to reread the three paragraphs and use them to answer the true-false items. *Part B:* Discuss the pay slip and help students understand it. Then assign the completion items.

90

Paying Taxes

Jim Jones, Pat Smith, and Ted King all live and work in the same state. They pay a federal and a state income tax. They pay excise tax on the cars they own. In this state, the more the car is worth, the more excise tax the owner must pay. Jim, Pat, and Ted all went shopping this week and each made a new purchase. This state has a sales tax of 5%. The sales tax is added to the price on the price tag. **Look at the chart, then answer the questions below.**

	Jim Jones	Pat Smith	Ted King
Salary	$24,000	$27,000	$20,000
Income Tax (approx.)	$2,900	$3,700	$2,300
Car Excise Tax	1980 Ford $10 a year	1983 Ford $150 a year	1988 Ford $400 a year
New Purchase	TV—$300	sofa—$600	boat—$8,000

Answer these questions with complete sentences. The first one is done for you.

1. If you were Jim Jones, how much money would you make a year?
   If I were Jim, I'd (I would) make $24,000 a year.

2. If you were Pat Smith, about how much income tax would you pay?

3. If you made $20,000 a year, about how much income tax would you pay?

4. If you owned Pat's car, how old would your car be? _____
   How much would you pay in car excise tax? _____

5. If you owned a 1980 Ford, how old would your car be? _____
   How much car excise tax would you pay? _____

6. If you owned a 1989 Ford, would you pay more or less excise tax than Ted?

7. If you bought the same color TV as Jim, how much sales tax (5%) would you pay?

8. If you bought the same sofa as Pat did, how much sales tax (5%) would you pay? What would be the total bill? _____

9. If you bought all three purchases shown here, the TV, the sofa and the boat, how much would your total bill be, including the 5% sales tax? _____

Skill Objectives: Understanding taxes; answering *if* questions; reading a chart; solving mathematical word problems. Review the concept of taxes. Explain that an excise tax is paid each year, but a sales tax is paid only at the time something is bought. Point out the construction *If I were* in the sample answer. Allow time for students to read the chart and ask questions about it, then assign the page for independent work.

91

Your Income Tax

Every year, people working in the United States must report their earnings to the Internal Revenue Service, the IRS. This is the government's tax office. The report is called an Income Tax Return. One form is shown on the next page. Separate instructions explain how to fill it out. Forms can be picked up at the bank or an IRS office. You can pay an accountant to fill out your tax return, or you can do it yourself.

Most wage earners get a yearly W-2 form (Wage and Tax Statement) from their employers. This form states how much the worker has earned and how much money has been withheld from, or already taken out of, the worker's pay for taxes. You must attach a copy of this W-2 form to your Income Tax Return form.

A. Read the W-2 form below. Use the figures to complete Binh Tran's Income Tax Return (Form 1040EZ) shown on the next page. Write in Binh's address and Social Security number, then fill in the necessary information on lines 1–11.

Words and Meanings

interest—money paid you by a bank if you have a savings account
charitable contributions—money given to a church or other non-profit organization
exemptions, deductions—allowances that lower the taxes you must pay
refund—money returned to you

B. Use the Tax Return form on page 93 to answer these questions. Circle your answers.

1. The 1040EZ form is for:
   a. a married person with children   b. a single person with children
   c. a single person with no children or other dependents

2. Line 1 has Binh's salary for the year. Binh earned more than his salary because:
   a. he has a savings account   b. he owned stock in a company
   c. he worked overtime

3. If you are single and are not claimed on anyone else's tax return, your standard deduction and personal exemption amount to:
   a. $6,556.00   b. $5,100.00   c. $32,000.00

4. Which statement is true?
   a. Binh owes the IRS more money.   b. The IRS owes Binh a refund.
   c. Binh doesn't owe the government any money and the government doesn't owe him any money.

5. At the bottom of the 1040EZ form, you are asked to sign your name after this statement: "Under penalty of perjury, I declare that to the best of my knowledge and belief, the return is correct and complete." What does the phrase, "Under penalty of perjury" mean in this sentence?
   a. Having followed the instructions above   b. In complete privacy
   c. Knowing the punishment for lying

Skill Objectives: Understanding taxes; locating specific information; completing a form. Tell students that this page is to be used in conjunction with page 93. Review the concept of income tax (page 90). Read the first two paragraphs with the class and discuss the words in the box. Then assign Part A. Students use the completed form on page 93 to do Part B.

92

Form
1040EZ

**Income Tax Return for
Single Filers With No Dependents** (5)

**Name &
address**

Use the IRS mailing label. If you don't have one, please print.

Please print your numbers like this:

$9\ 8\ 7\ 6\ 5\ 4\ 3\ 2\ 1\ 0$

L
A
B
E
L

H
E
R
E

Binh N. Tran
Print your name above (first, initial, last)

Home address (number and street). (If you have a P.O. box, see back.)   Apt. no.

City, town or post office, state, and ZIP code

Your social security number

**Instructions are on the back. Also, see the Form 1040A/
1040EZ booklet, especially the checklist on page 14.**

Presidential Election Campaign Fund
Do you want $1 to go to this fund?

*Note: Checking "Yes" will
not change your tax or
reduce your refund.* ▶

Yes No

☑

Dollars   Cents

**Report
your
income**

Attach
Copy B of
Form(s)
W-2 here.

*Note: You
must check
Yes or No.*

1   Total wages, salaries, and tips. This should be shown in Box 10
of your W-2 form(s). (Attach your W-2 form(s).)   **1**

2   Taxable interest income of $400 or less. If the total is more
than $400, you cannot use Form 1040EZ.   **2**

| 1 | 8 | 0 | . | | |

3   Add line 1 and line 2. This is your **adjusted gross income.**   **3**

4   Can your parents (or someone else) claim you on their return?
☐ **Yes.** Do worksheet on back; enter amount from line E here.
☐ **No.** Enter 5,100. This is the total of your standard
deduction and personal exemption.   **4**

| 5 | 1 | 0 | 0 | . | | |

5   Subtract line 4 from line 3. If line 4 is larger than line 3,
enter 0. This is your **taxable income.**   **5**

**Figure
your
tax**

6   Enter your Federal income tax withheld from Box 9 of your
W-2 form(s).   **6**

7   **Tax.** Use the amount on **line 5** to look up your tax in the tax
table on pages 41-46 of the Form 1040A/1040EZ booklet. Use
the **single** column in the table. Enter the tax from the table on
this line.   **7**

| 5 | 1 | 2 | 8 | . | | |

**Refund
or
amount
you owe**

Attach tax
payment here.

8   If line 6 is larger than line 7, subtract line 7 from line 6.
This is your **refund.**   **8**

9   If line 7 is larger than line 6, subtract line 6 from line 7. This
is the **amount you owe.** Attach check or money order for
the full amount, payable to "Internal Revenue Service."   **9**

**Sign
your
return**

(Keep a copy
of this form
for your
records.)

I have read this return. Under penalties of perjury, I declare
that to the best of my knowledge and belief, the return is true,
correct, and complete.

Your signature   Date

X   *Binh N. Tran*   3/4

For IRS Use Only—Please
do not write in boxes below.

Skill Objectives: Completing a form; understanding taxes. See annotation for page 92. If these pages are done during the tax season
(January through April 15), you may wish to obtain additional forms from a bank or income tax office and have students fill them in with information about themselves (if they have income) or with data supplied by you. Extension: Pass out copies of the more complicated Forms 1040A and
1040 and discuss the kinds of information requested.

Reading the Newspaper: Help Wanted

The "Help Wanted" (job) ads are found in the Classified section of the newspaper, along with real estate listings, apartments for rent, second-hand car listings, and ads for other things people want to sell. "Help Wanted" ads are often divided into several categories, for example, Sales Openings, General Help, Business Help, Medical Help, and Professional Help. The ads on this page were selected from all five categories. As you read the "want ads" below, decide under which heading each belongs.

SECRETARY

Full-time oppty. to work in warm, friendly but busy professional office in Central Business District. You will help with filing, typing, answering the telephone, etc. Requires high school education, excellent appearance, pleasant personality, typing ability + willingness to work at varied duties. Would consider person re-entering work force if can still type. Salary open. Please send resume and letter explaining background and qualifications to Ms. Joan Foster, 2 Main Street, San Diego, CA 92109.

WRECKER DRIVERS FULL OR PART TIME

Must have good driving record, all benefits. Apply:
MAL'S
7 Mass. Ave., Lincolnville

ESL INSTRUCTORS
F.T./P.T., DAYS/EVES.

1) Attleboro/Fall River, full time, now... (2) Various Southeast CA locations, part time... Resumes:
URBANISTICS, 33 N. Main St., Handels, CA 92991

Training Opportunity for
NURSE AIDES
7–3:30 Only

Six month training program. Upon completion, certificate issued & full time permanent position. 40 hours weekly & benefits.

Send resume and cover letter to:

**PERSONNEL OFFICE
ELIHU WAITE NURSING &
REHABILITATION CENTER
HARRIS COVE 92931**

RETAIL
INFANT TO TEEN

A BETTER CHILDREN'S APPAREL STORE

STORE MANAGERS
ASSISTANT MANAGERS
SALESPERSONS

Top salary and benefits for the qualified.

Send resume to Dept. BT,
LITTLE FOLKS SHOP
Div. ABC Shoe Corp.
Executive Office
Rte. 337
Charlesville, IL 69999

AUTOMOTIVE CAREERS

You must be able to work in a progressive, fast moving automotive service organization. We need mature, serious, professional, responsible hard workers with strong desire to succeed to work as Service Advisors. Must enjoy customer contact & technical decision making. Contact for appointment Roy Chevrolet, Rte. 114, Denville.

WORD PROCESSOR OPER.

Phelps Press seeks 2 exp. operators to process text of current books and magazines and translate them into braille on our specialized computer system. Requirements are exc. typing and spelling, proficiency with the English language and an interest in learning braille. Gd. benefits. Starting salary $12,480-15,000. Send resume to: Phelps Press Inc., 88 St. Basil's St., Wrightsville Falls.

TELLERS

Work on beautiful Cape Cod in a new community Federal Credit Union. Excellent salary and benefits.
Please send resume to:
FEDERAL CREDIT UNION
Box 62, Wrightsville

COMPUTER SALES

Join the world's fastest growing chain of retail computer stores. You must be a sales pro with superior communication skills. Accounting, small-business or computer background helpful, but not required. College degree a must. Earning potential unlimited. We are a people-oriented company with excellent benefits.

Send resume in confidence.
No phone calls, please

Computer City

4 Henshaw St., Dale City 92929

RENTAL AGENT

Part time energetic Rental Agent wanted for a fast growing development. Please send resume to: BELPORT HISTORIC ASSOC., 100 Captains Row, Belport.

SOLAR

Expanding solar manufacturer has several immediate openings in service installation and sales departments. No experience required. We provide complete training. High starting pay plus many benefits. No layoffs.
CALL 532-6622

PRODUCTION INVENTORY CONTROL CLERK

Well estab. manufacturer & distributor. Immed. opening. Growth oppty. to also learn purchasing. Accuracy w/ details & figures a must. Apply w/ resume to: V88 Times Office, Wrightsville Times, Wrightsville 92899.

A. Some job advertisements ask applicants to call for an interview appointment. Others ask applicants to send a resume (rez′ə mā) explaining their background and qualifications for the job. The employer looks through all the resumes, selects the best qualified applicants, and then asks those people to come in for a personal interview. At the interview, the employer asks questions such as those below. **Choose a "want ad" from above that interests you. On a separate piece of paper, write answers to the questions below. For #6, feel free to ask the employer any questions you'd like answered. Next, practice the interview with a partner. Your partner, who is playing the employer, must answer the questions you ask in #6.**

1. Why are you interested in this job?

2. Have you ever had a job before? If so, what was it?

3. What special qualifications do you have for this job?

4. What are you doing at present?

5. When could you begin this job?

6. Are there any questions you'd like to ask me about this job?

Skill Objectives: Reading for detail; classifying; interpreting help-wanted ads; role playing. Read and discuss the introductory paragraph. Give students time to read the ads, then discuss the heading under which each would be found. *Part A:* If possible, allow each student to role play both the employer's and the employee's part. Individuals who feel confident about their English may perform their interviews for the class.

B. A resume gives concise information about your background, your work experience, your education, and your interests. It is a good idea to bring your resume with you to a job interview. Sometimes the interviewer will ask to see it. The information on the resume will help you fill out the job application forms.

It is important that your resume look neat and well organized, and that the information be easy to read. It should be typewritten on a single sheet of paper.

Look at the resume at the right. Notice how Andrea has set up the resume and the type of information she has given.

Choose a "want ad" from page 94 that interests you. On a separate sheet of paper write your own resume, following the form shown here. Under Experience, list your most recent job first. Under Education, list your most recent school first.

```
                           RESUME

                      Andrea Villarosa
                      769 Everett Street
                  San Diego, California 92110
                     Telephone: 441-8864

Position Desired:   Secretary

Experience:         Clerk-typist              Summers
                    Milton Hospital           1988-1989
                    San Diego, CA

                    Babysitter/Mother's helper  After school
                    Mrs. Janet Richman          and weekends,
                    323 San Mateo Rd.           1987-1990
                    San Diego, CA

                    Library assistant          1985-1986
                    (volunteer)
                    Central Jr. High
                    San Diego, CA

Education:          San Diego High School      1987-1990
                    (Commercial course)

                    Central Jr. High           1984-1987
                    San Diego, CA

                    South Central Elementary   1977-1984
                    San Diego, CA

Special Abilities:  Bilingual in Spanish and English

Awards and          ''Outstanding Business Student''  1990
Activities:         Captain, Girl's Basketball Team    1989-1990
                    Cheerleader                        1988-1990
```

C. When you send a resume, you also have to send a cover letter to introduce yourself and interest your potential employer. Study the sample cover letter below. **On a separate piece of paper, write a similar cover letter to go with your resume. Tell your potential employer which job you are applying for and briefly mention your strongest qualifications. Before closing, express your interest in meeting for an interview.**

```
                                    769 Everett Street
                                    San Diego, California 92110
                                    June 1, 1990

Ms. Joan Foster
Data Systems, Inc.
22 Main Street
San Diego, California 92109

Dear Ms. Foster:

     I am answering your ad in the "Patriot Herald"
for a secretary.  I am graduating from San Diego High
School this month.  I was just named "Outstanding
Business Student."  My previous work experience includes
two summers as a clerk-typist at Milton Hospital.

     I would like to come in and talk with you about
the position of secretary with your company.  I am
enclosing my resume with more information about myself.

                              Sincerely,

                              Andrea Villarosa
                              Andrea Villarosa
```

Skill Objectives: Writing a resume; writing a cover letter. Read and discuss the first two paragraphs. Emphasize the importance of neatness and accuracy in a resume. Discuss the term *cover letter* (also called *covering letter*) and stress that this, too, must be neat and correctly phrased and spelled. Elicit that a carelessly prepared resume or letter suggests that the applicant may be generally careless and may lose him or her a job. Then assign Parts B and C. Have students exchange and discuss their resumes and letters.

Figure It Out!

Read the problems below, then answer the questions. Use the space provided on the right to do the necessary math work. The first question is done for you.

1. You and your friend are in a restaurant in Boston. Your bill comes to $50.00. In Massachusetts, there is a 5% meal tax on restaurant meals.

   a. How much meal tax must you pay? _____$2.50_____

   b. What will the total bill be? _____

   $$\begin{array}{r} \$50 \quad (bill) \\ \times .05 \quad (\times 5\%) \\ \hline \$2.50 = meal\ tax \end{array}$$

2. You are in the same restaurant in Boston. This time your bill, including the meal tax, comes to $82.00. Usually, people leave their waitress or waiter a 15% tip.

   a. How much tip should you leave? _____

   b. How much wil you spend on the meal, including the tip? _____

3. George's godmother has just left him $4,000 in her will. In Oregon, where George lives, the state charges a 12% inheritance tax.

   a. How much tax must George pay? _____

   b. How much money will he have left, after paying the inheritance tax? _____

4. Mr. Pappas bought a new Ford Escort last month. He paid $7300 for it. Mr. Pappas lives in a state where the sales tax is 8%.

   a. How much sales tax did he pay? _____

   b. What was the total cost of the car? _____

5. Mrs. Gonzales makes $41,000 a year. This year, all wage owners must pay 7.65% of their salary to Social Security.

   How much will Mrs. Gonzales pay towards Social Security this year? _____

6. Carolina took a taxi from the airport to her apartment. The price was $15.50. People usually figure a 15% tip for the driver, add the tip to the fee, then pay the driver the nearest round amount.

   How much did Carolina probably give the driver? _____

7. Mr. and Mrs. Ayala own a house in Rexford. The value of the house is $210,000. The property tax in Rexford is 2.5% of the property value.

   How much do the Ayalas pay in property taxes every year? _____

Skill Objectives: Solving mathematical word problems; computing percents; understanding taxes. Discuss percents and make sure students understand how to compute a particular percent (5% of $2.00 equals .05 times $2.00 or 10 cents). Elicit that 1 percent is equal to 1/100 (one one-hundredth). Have students read through the problems and mark unfamiliar terms. Explain the terms and assign the page. Let individual students put their work on the board and explain their methods. (Answers are on page 125.)

Finding the Job

Here are some more Help Wanted ads. These jobs were listed in the Classified section under the heading "General Help." **Read the ads, then answer the questions below.**

AUTOPARTS COUNTER PERSON Must be experienced. Alltown area. 379-0065, ask for Joe.

CLERK TYPIST Bi-lingual, must be fast accurate typist. Good phone personality with Spanish/English customers. Excellent benefits. Jill Wagner 724-0568

COUNTER PERSON Dry cleaning store. Full time 7–3. 337-4445

DELIVERY/MESSENGER Person with own car to work for downtown law firm. $275/wk + travel expenses. Call Office Manager, 758-0722

DESK CLERK All shifts, full and part time. Brewster Hotel. Call Jean Stall, 734-6672

NEWSPAPER CARRIERS Openings for permanent part time carriers M–F, 4 a.m.–8 a.m. Must have reliable vehicle. Salary $6.50 per hr. Please call btwn 8 a.m. and noon only for appt. 333-1218

MECHANICS Dealership needs mechanics for day and night shifts. Excellent pay and benefits. For information, stop in. Ask for Service Manager. Allen's Ford, 40 Jay St., Newtown

SECURITY GUARDS Full and part time in and around Newtown area. Many positions available. Must be 21 yrs. or over with H.S. diploma. ALPHA SECURITY, 10:30–4:30. Call 367-4255

SERVICE STATION ATTENDANT Clean, neat, personable. Apply Wed. May 14, 520 Northover Pike, Lincoln

TRAVEL AGENT for our Eastwood office. Computer knowledge essential, pref. SABRE. Please contact Mr. Ferris, Apex Travel, 367-4897

A. 1. Name two jobs you can apply for in person. _____

_____

2. Name two jobs for which you need your own car. _____

_____

3. Name one job requiring computer knowledge. _____

4. Name one job for which you must be a high school graduate. _____

5. What type of work would the dry cleaning counter person do? _____

_____

6. What sort of experience would the autoparts counter person need? Why?

_____

7. What would the duties of the hotel desk clerk be? _____

_____

8. What would the duties of the security guard be? _____

_____

B. Many of these ads ask you to call for an interview appointment. When you call, the employer will probably ask you some questions over the phone. **Choose one job to call for an interview. Complete the conversation below on a separate piece of paper, then practice the telephone dialogue with a partner.**

Employer: Hello, this is _____. Can I help you?

You:

Employer: Do you have any work experience?

You:

Employer:

You:

Employer: Can you begin work immediately?

You:

Employer: When can you come in for an interview?

You:

Employer: All right. Thank you for calling. We'll see you then.

Preparing for Tests:
Stated and Implied Ideas (2)

Hawaii, the newest state in the United States, is a group of eight large islands and many small ones in the Central Pacific Ocean, about 2,000 miles west of San Francisco.

Hawaii was probably first settled about A.D. 750 by seafarers from other Pacific islands. The first Europeans or Americans to visit it were the British Captain James Cook and his crew in 1778. Cook named his discovery the Sandwich Islands after the sponsor of his expedition, the Earl of Sandwich. Twelve years later, others from Europe and the new United States began to settle in the islands.

These "westerners" brought trouble to Hawaii. They brought new diseases, which the Hawaiians had no immunity to, they brought alcohol, to which many Hawaiians became addicted, and they brought a new religion which uprooted the old values and forced the islanders to abandon their native culture and conform to a new one.

Many Americans settled in Hawaii, and in 1893 they overthrew the queen and made Hawaii a republic. Sanford Dole, a missionary's son, was made president. In 1898, the United States annexed, or took over the islands, and they became a territory of the United States in 1900.

On December 7, 1941, the Japanese bombed Pearl Harbor, Hawaii. This attack brought about the entrance of the United States into World War II. In 1959, the United States Congress admitted Hawaii to statehood, making it the fiftieth state in the United States. For the first time in almost 200 years, Hawaiians were able to participate in the electoral process.

Circle the best answer for each question.

1. Hawaii was originally named the Sandwich Islands because
   a. it was "sandwiched" between other Pacific islands
   b. the Earl of Sandwich discovered it
   c. James Cook named it for his sponsor, the Earl of Sandwich
   d. Captain Cook ate the first sandwich on the islands

2. "Western" settlement on the islands was
   a. helpful to the natives living on the islands
   b. helpful to "westerners" who caught several diseases from the islanders
   c. thwarted by seafarers for twelve years
   d. harmful to the indigenous population of the islands

3. Sanford Dole became president of Hawaii
   a. when the queen abdicated her throne
   b. by order of the U.S. President
   c. in a democratic election of the Hawaiian people
   d. when the reigning queen was overthrown

4. Which of the following represent a logical conclusion about the Hawaiian natives in the 19th century?
   a. Most who died did so from diseases brought by "westerners."
   b. They clung stubbornly to their religion.
   c. They were able to control alcohol very well.
   d. They approved of European encroachment of their islands.

Skill Objectives: Reading for inference; finding specific information; drawing conclusions. Explain to students that this exercise is typical of those found on standardized tests. Remind them of the importance of reading carefully but quickly. You may want to give them a time limit—six minutes is suggested—to accustom them to pacing themselves. After they have completed the exercise, reread the passage orally and have students take turns answering the questions; discuss/explain all answers, paying special attention to the inference questions.

98

Dear Dot

Dear Dot—

I am a boy and I would like to be a nurse. I don't tell many people that because even my closest friends laugh at me when I tell them, but it is true. My uncle is a male nurse and he is a great guy and his job sounds great. I want to be like him, and I want to be part of the medical profession. Even my family says that I should try to be a doctor, but that's not what I want. I want to be a nurse. What can I tell my friends and family so that they will leave me alone?

Bugged

Discuss each of the questions in class. Then write your answers.

1. Why do people laugh when Bugged says he wants to be a nurse? _____
   _____

2. Do you think there is such a thing as a woman's profession or a man's profession? Why or why not? _____
   _____

3. What are the advantages of being a nurse rather than a doctor? _____
   _____

4. Do you think Bugged's family should try to persuade him to be a doctor? Why or why not?
   _____
   _____

5. What can Bugged say to the people who question his career choice? _____
   _____
   _____

Write About It

Now put yourself in Dot's place. Write a helpful answer to Bugged. Remember, you want to help solve the problem, not make fun of the writer or criticize him.

Dear Bugged—

_____

_____

_____

_____

_____

_____

_____

_____

Skill Objectives: Reading for main idea and details; making inferences and judgments; expressing opinions in writing. Read the letter aloud (or have a student read it). Discuss each question in class. Encourage freedom of expression, but be sure students can support their opinions. Then have students write answers to the questions. Suggest they use these answers as the basis for their letters. You may wish to assign the letter-writing activity as homework.

99

I Wish I Could

A. Sonya and Raul recently moved from Santo Domingo to St. Paul, Minnesota. They are having some problems in their new surroundings.

1. They can't find good jobs.
2. They can't get used to American food.
3. They can't figure out the money system.
4. They can't speak English well.
5. They can't get used to the cold weather.

Sonya and Raul wish that they could do all these things. If they could, they would be much happier.

Look at the five problems listed above. What do Sonya and Raul wish they could do? Answer with five complete sentences. The first one is done for you.

1. _They wish that they could find good jobs._
2. _____
3. _____
4. _____
5. _____

B. Here are some other problems that Sonya and Raul are having.

1. They don't <u>have</u> much money.
2. They don't have a car.
3. There isn't much heat in their apartment.
4. Their upstairs neighbors are very noisy.
5. They have a very small apartment.

What do Sonya and Raul wish? Answer with five complete sentences. Use the past tense for the second verb. The first one is done for you.

1. _They wish that they <u>had</u> more money._
2. _____
3. _____
4. _____
5. _____

C. **Complete the following sentences, using *would* or *could*.** The first two are done for you. Use them as models.

1. If Sonya and Raul could find good jobs, _they would have more money_ .
2. If they spoke better English, _they could make more friends_ .
3. If they had a car, _____ .
4. If they could figure out the money system, _____ .
5. If they had a bigger apartment, _____ .
6. If their upstairs neighbors were quieter, _____ .

Skill Objectives: Using *wish* conditional; completing conditional sentences. Write *They can't find good jobs.* on the board; under it write *They wish that they could find good jobs.* Discuss the structural changes and the change in verb tense; do the same with the first sentence of Part B, then assign both parts for independent work. *Part C:* Discuss the difference in meaning between *could* and *would*; elicit that either one may fit in some sentences. Then assign as written work.

100

Madeline Madden

Madeline Madden is mad at everyone and everything. Why is she mad? Well, . . .

Her son never cleans his bedroom.
Her daughter never helps around the house.
Her husband works until 8:00 every night.
It's been raining for four days.
Her mother calls her every morning and every night.

It's too much!

A. What does Madeline wish? Answer in complete sentences.
The first one is done for you.

1. _She wishes that her son would clean his bedroom._

2. _____

3. _____

4. _____

5. _____

B. Who do you get mad at? What do you wish they would do? What do you wish they wouldn't do?

1. _____

2. _____

3. _____

C. Read the situations below. What do these people wish that they had done? Answer the questions with complete sentences. Use the past perfect tense in your answer. The first one is done for you. Use it as a model.

1. Madeline never <u>went</u> to college. Now she can't find a job that she likes. Everyone says, "You need a college education for this job."

   What does she wish? _She wishes that she <u>had</u> <u>gone</u> to college._

2. Madeline's son, Robert, never studied much when he was in high school. He was not accepted at any of the colleges he applied to.

   What does he wish now? _____

3. Madeline's daughter, Rosa, always spent her money on clothes, and never saved a dime. Now she can't afford to take a vacation in Miami with her girlfriends.

   What does she wish? _____

4. Madeline and her husband went to France last month. They didn't take any French lessons before they went, and couldn't communicate with anyone.

   What do they wish they had done? _____

   _____

Skill Objectives: *Wish* **conditional with past and past perfect tenses; expressing wishes in writing.** Read the anecdotal paragraph with the class. Make sure students understand the directions for Part A. Review the structural changes in the sample sentence, then assign. *Part B:* Discuss what students are "mad at," and elicit sample answers; assign as written work. *Part C:* Note the tense shift from past to past perfect in the sample sentence (*never went, wishes that she had gone*). Assign as written work.

101

What Did You Say?

A. Answer the questions below. The first one is done for you. Notice that the verb *will* in the quoted speech is changed to *would* in the reported speech.

1. Martha said, "I <u>will</u> meet you in the cafeteria."
   What did she say? *She said that she <u>would</u> meet me in the cafeteria.*

2. Paul and Ronnie said, "We will come to the party."
   What did they say? _____

3. My father said, "I will be in Washington, D.C., next week."
   What did he say? _____

4. The President said, "I will stop pollution."
   What did he say? _____

5. The teacher said, "I will give you a test next Monday."
   What did she say? _____

6. I said, "I will pay the rent next week."
   What did I say? _____

7. We said, "We will take care of everything."
   What did we say? _____

B. Answer the questions below. The first one is done for you. Notice that the past tense or present perfect verb in the quoted speech is changed to the past perfect in the reported speech.

1. My sister said, "I <u>saw</u> that movie last week."
   What did she say? *She said that she <u>had seen</u> that movie last week.*

2. The weather reporters said, "The weather was sunny all last week."
   What did they say? _____

3. The newscaster said, "The police caught the robber."
   What did she say? _____

4. The teacher said, "I forgot to correct your homework."
   What did he say? _____

5. The President said, "I have reduced taxes."
   What did he say? _____

6. They said, "We have already eaten dinner."
   What did they say? _____

7. You said, "I have finally finished doing my homework."
   What did you say? _____

Skill Objective: Reported speech with past and past perfect tenses. Discuss the difference between direct quotation and reported speech (indirect quotation). Point out the grammatical change from *will* to *would* (Part A), and from simple past to past perfect (Part B). Do the entire page orally with the class before assigning as written work.

102

Too, Very, Enough

Three frequently used words in English sentences are *too, very,* and *enough*. Look at the following sentence to see how each is used: "Martha was *very* tall, tall *enough* to stand out in a crowd, and *too* tall to wear most of the clothes in the store." **Read the discussion below of these three words.**

VERY *Very* is called an *intensifier* because it intensifies (makes stronger) the word that follows it. Example: She was intelligent/She was <u>very</u> intelligent.

TOO *Too* is also an intensifier, but it goes beyond *very*. *Too* means more than is wanted or needed. Example: "He is <u>too</u> young to go to school" means that he is younger than is needed to go to school. *Too* gives a negative meaning to a sentence. "Too young to go to school" means one can't go to school.

ENOUGH *Enough* means the right amount. In these two sentences, *enough* modifies nouns. "There's <u>enough</u> food for everyone." "We don't have <u>enough</u> time."
  Enough can also modify or change the meaning of adjectives. When you use an adjective + *enough* + an infinitive, you are saying that something is possible—that it can be done. Example: "He is tall <u>enough</u> to play basketball." When *enough* is used to modify an adjective in a negative statement, it has the opposite meaning: something is impossible, cannot be done. Example: "He is <u>not</u> tall <u>enough</u> to play basketball."

Now complete the sentences. Put *too, very,* or *enough* in each blank.

1. Mr. Smith is 84; he's _____ old to find a job.

2. Mrs. Getty is rich _____ to buy anything she wants.

3. Do you have _____ money to buy that bicycle?

4. San Francisco is a _____ beautiful city.

5. My daughter is _____ young to drive a car.

6. Susanna can't play basketball, she's _____ short.

7. George is 18. Is he old _____ to get married?

8. I am _____ sorry to hear about your accident.

9. Miami is _____ nice but it is _____ hot in the summer.

10. I don't like living in Canada; it's _____ cold.

11. There wasn't _____ snow, so we couldn't go skiing.

12. My car is _____ beautiful, but it uses _____ much gasoline.

13. Karl is smart _____ to go to any college he wants.

14. I don't have _____ energy to go jogging today.

15. Chinese is a _____ difficult language to learn.

16. My father was _____ sick to go to work yesterday.

17. It isn't warm _____ to go to the beach today.

18. I don't like chocolate; it's _____ sweet.

Skill Objective: Using quantifying adverbs. Many students find *too, very,* and *enough* extremely difficult. Read and discuss the introductory paragraphs and be sure the students understand what each of the three words means. Assign the page for written work; when students have finished, review and discuss the answers in class.

103

The Bill of Rights: Basic Freedoms

As you know, the Constitution of the United States is the plan for the American Government. When it was written, in 1787, it was sent to the states for approval. Two-thirds of the states had to approve it.

Many people liked the Constitution and wanted to have it approved immediately. Others, however, said that they would not approve it unless a list of the rights held by the people was attached to it. Such a "bill of rights" was part of most of the state constitutions, and these people believed strongly that the national Constitution should also have one.

Americans wanted their rights listed because, before the Revolution, the English government had taken away rights that the people believed they had. They did not want their new national government to do the same thing. They wanted to limit its power.

Because of this, the very first session of Congress, in 1789, proposed a series of amendments (changes) that listed rights that the people had. Ten of these amendments were ratified (approved) by the states and are known as the Bill of Rights.

Here are the rights that the first ten amendments give all Americans. Keep in mind that these rights apply to the national government, not to the state governments. Many of them, however, have been *extended* or *applied* to the states as well as to the national government.

1. The first amendment says that there will be no official, national religion, and that people can practice whatever religion they choose. It also says that people can say what they want to say and print what they want to print. It says that they can meet together peacefully and protest anything they think is unfair.

2. The second amendment says that the national government cannot stop people from keeping arms (guns, etc.). (This amendment was written to make sure that "militias" or citizen armies would be ready to defend the people.)

3. The third amendment forbids the government to force people to let soldiers live in their houses in peacetime. (The English had made people do this in the years before the Revolution.)

4. The fourth amendment says that police officers must have a warrant—an order from a judge—before they can search a person's house or property or before they can take away any thing or any person. The warrant must tell exactly what place is to be searched, and what or who is to be taken.

5. The fifth amendment guarantees that a person will get a fair trial. It says that nobody can be forced to give evidence against himself or herself, and that nobody can be imprisoned or put to death unless that person has been tried and convicted by a court that follows the laws of the United States. It also says that if the government has to take away a person's land or house, it must pay the person a fair price.

6. The sixth amendment says that a person who has been accused of a crime has a right to a speedy trial, in public, by a jury. It says that the person will be told exactly what he or she is accused of and will know who is testifying against him or her. It also says that the person is entitled to call witnesses and to have a lawyer.

7. The seventh amendment guarantees that a person can have a trial by jury in cases where there is no crime but where one person is suing another.

8. The eighth amendment says that cruel or unusual punishments will not be given to a person. It says that he or she cannot be forced to pay unreasonably high fines or bail. (Bail is money that is paid to guarantee that a person will be in court for his or her trial. If the person does not come to court, the bail becomes the property of the government. If he or she does come to court, the bail is returned.)

9. The ninth amendment says that the people have many other rights besides those listed. It says that just because a right isn't listed doesn't mean that it is less important than those that are listed.

10. The tenth amendment says that any powers that are not given to the national government by the Constitution or that are not prohibited to the states by the Constitution belong to the states or to the people. This means that the national government cannot suddenly take powers that are not listed or implied in the Constitution.

(Go on to the next page.)

Skill Objectives: Reading for main ideas and details; building vocabulary. Before reading the article, ask students what they know about the Bill of Rights. Do they know of other countries that provide a similar guarantee of freedoms? Preview the following vocabulary: *approval, proposed, amendments, ratified, protest, forbid, guarantee, accused, testify, suing, jury, prohibit.* Then assign the page for independent reading and provide help as needed.

Read the article on the previous page and use it to answer the questions and do the exercises below.

1. Why did many people demand that a bill of rights should be added to the Constitution? (Circle your answer.)

   a. They were afraid that the English would take away their rights.
   b. They knew that the state constitutions had bills of rights.
   c. They wanted to limit the power of the national government.
   d. They wanted to strengthen what the national government could do.

2. Which amendment says that you do not have to answer a question in court if you think the answer could be evidence against you?

   _____

3. If a police officer asks to search your house, what must he or she have? (Circle your answer.)

   a. bail   b. a fair price   c. a plan   d. a warrant

4. Which amendment guarantees freedom of the press?

   _____

5. Which amendment says that you can call a meeting to protest something that the government is doing?

   _____

6. In 1789, when the Bill of Rights was written, the third amendment was considered to be very important. However, it has never been used. Why was it thought to be important then? Why did it turn out not to be important? (Use more paper if you need to.)

   _____
   _____
   _____
   _____
   _____

7. The first eight amendments all forbid the national government to do things, or guarantee that it will do certain things that it might not otherwise do. Why do you think the people wanted to put such limits on the government? (Use more paper for your answer if you need to.)

   _____
   _____
   _____
   _____
   _____

8. Read the ninth amendment. On your paper list some important rights that Americans have that are not in the Bill of Rights.

Skill Objectives: Locating specific information; drawing conclusions; making inferences; writing paragraphs. After the students complete the reading on page 104, assign this page for independent work. Allow class time for oral discussions of students' answers. Provide a copy of the Bill of Rights in its original language for students to refer to. Extension: Have students research the campaign to get the Constitution ratified.

105

Reading the Newspaper: Real Estate

In some newspapers, Real Estate is listed in the Index as a separate section. In other papers, the Real Estate section is included in the Classified section. The Real Estate section contains advertisements for houses and apartments that are for sale or rent. A special language is used in real estate ads—the language of abbreviations. The box below lists some of the most common real estate abbreviations. Use the dictionary to look up any unfamiliar words.

apt.	apartment	elev.	elevator	kit.	kitchen	renov.	renovated
avail.	available	fl.	floor	lge.	large	rm.	room
bdrm.	bedroom	furn.	furnished	mod.	modern	std.	studio
bldg.	building	gar.	garage	mo.	month	stv.	stove
dinrm.	diningroom	htd.	heated	nec.	necessary	util.	utilities
dep.	deposit	hw.	hot water	pkg.	parking	ww.	wall-to-wall carpet
dw.	dishwasher	incl.	included	refrig.	refrigerator	yd.	yard

A. Rewrite the real estate advertisements below in unabbreviated English.

Afton—Lge. mod. apt. 2-bdrm. ww. dw. gar. $680 mo. 763-0496.

_____

_____

Newton—Std. 3rd fl. elev. mod. bldg. htd. $795 mo. 944-3201 after 5 pm.

_____

_____

Cranford—6 rm. renov. dinrm. lge. kit. Ht/hw. incl. $485 mo. 962-4400.

_____

_____

Everett—3 rm. apt. all util. Private pkg. Avail. 6/1 Dep. nec. $600 mo. 339-3876.

_____

_____

B. Rewrite these advertisements in abbreviated form.

Arlington—Furnished apartment, two bedrooms, large kitchen, nice yard. No utilities. $850 a month. 442-1197.

_____

_____

Concord—One room apartment, wall-to-wall carpeting. Heated, modern building. Available May 1. $450 a month. 942-7601.

_____

_____

Berlin—Modern two bedroom apartment, fourth floor in renovated building. New stove and refrigerator. Heat and hot water included. $800 a month. 665-4311.

_____

_____

C. Now, write an advertisement for an apartment you would like to rent. Use real estate abbreviations.

_____

_____

Skill Objectives: Interpreting real estate advertising; understanding and using abbreviations. Read the introductory paragraph. Allow sufficient time for students to familiarize themselves with the abbreviations in the box. Go over the directions for each of the three parts, and be sure students understand what they are to do; then assign the page for independent work. Extension: Have students get real estate ads from local newspapers and compare the rents on this page with those in their own area.

106

D. The Real Estate section of a newspaper contains more than just ads for renting and buying. There are also articles about apartments and houses. **Read the following article, then answer the questions.**

LOOK BEFORE YOU LEAP

So, you're looking for your first apartment? This is a time for careful decisions. Don't be afraid of the realtor or landlord. Ask lots of questions. Find out as much as you can about your new home before you sign a lease and move in. Here are some important points to consider.

1. What is the noise level in the building? You may be living next door to a struggling trumpet player who practices until 3:00 a.m. Or you may love to play your saxophone late at night. Will there be problems? Are there young children in the building who cry all night? Ask questions. You may want to drive by the building late at night a couple of times during the week.

2. How is the electrical system? With old wiring you sometimes cannot run an air conditioner and a hair dryer at the same time without blowing a fuse. Make sure that the electrical system is right for your needs.

3. What about the windows? Do they open easily and close tightly? You'll be glad you checked this little detail out when the summer heat comes or a winter blizzard hits.

4. The kitchen can be a major problem area. Make sure that the sink drains properly and that the ceiling is in good shape. Dark patches or spots on the ceiling often indicate leaks from the kitchen above. While you're in the kitchen, check the refrigerator. Close the refrigerator door on a piece of paper. Let the paper stick out. If the paper falls out, then warm air is getting into the refrigerator. You will have higher electric bills and will need to defrost more often.

Go slowly when you are looking for a new apartment or house to rent. Check and recheck the facts. Make sure that it is the right place for you and that you are getting the most for your money.

1. What does the expression, "Look before you leap" mean? _____
   _____

2. *Tone* is the mood or attitude a writer communicates in his or her writing. What is the tone of this article?

   a. anxious, without much hope.   c. suspicious and angry
   b. comical and witty   d. cautious advice

3. What is a realtor? (Use a dictionary if you need to.) _____
   _____

4. What is a lease? _____

5. Why should you check the noise level of the apartment building? _____
   _____

6. What is often a problem with a weak electrical system? _____
   _____

7. What should you check for in the kitchen? _____
   _____
   _____

8. What additional advice would you give to new apartment renters? _____
   _____
   _____

Skill Objectives: Locating specific information; understanding figurative language; establishing tone. Read the introductory paragraph (or have it read) and emphasize that many newspapers carry articles about real estate as well as advertising. Have the article read, then discuss students' (and their families') experiences with houses or apartments. Reread the article aloud to help students establish tone. Then assign the questions for independent work.

107

Picture It

Discuss the two women in the picture with several classmates. Share your answers to the questions. Your ideas may be different: that's fine! Then write a paragraph about the picture on your own paper. Include your ideas about the five questions.

1. Who are these women?
2. Where are they?
3. What time of year is it? How are they dressed?
4. What are they talking about?
5. What is going to happen next?

Skill Objectives: Discussing and interpreting a photograph; writing a descriptive paragraph. Allow ample discussion of the women in the photograph. Encourage differences of opinion. Write important vocabulary on the board as it comes out in the discussion. Then have students write their paragraphs. (The photo shows a police officer trying to convince a homeless woman to come with her to a shelter; the picture was taken early in December.) Extension: bring in newspaper or magazine articles on the homeless, or have students do so. Read and discuss these before having the students write their paragraphs.

Dear Dot

Dear Dot—

Recently a boy named Mario sent his friend Rick to ask my girlfriend Suzy if I liked him (Mario). Suzy asked me and I said, "yes." She told Rick and Rick told Mario. Now Mario has asked me out on a date—sort of. He did the same thing as before. He asked his friend to ask my friend if I would go out with him. I said I wouldn't unless he asked me himself. He hasn't asked, and I would really like to go out on a date with him. Should I ask Suzy to ask Rick what happened?

Wondering

Discuss each of the questions in class. Then write your answers.

1. What is the correct way to ask someone out on a date? _____

_____

2. What does "mature" mean? _____

3. Do you think these students are being mature? Why or why not? _____

_____

4. Do you think Wondering was right to insist that Mario ask her out himself? Why or why not?

_____

_____

5. What do you think happened? _____

_____

6. What should Wondering do now? _____

_____

Write About It

Now put yourself in Dot's place. Write a helpful answer to Wondering. Remember, you want to help solve the problem, not make fun of the writer or criticize her.

Dear Wondering—

_____

_____

_____

_____

_____

_____

_____

_____

_____

_____

Skill Objectives: Reading for main idea; making judgments; predicting outcomes; expressing opinions in writing. Have students read the letter; be sure they understand the sequence described; you may want to have someone diagram it on the board. Discuss each question in class; point out that number 2 is a review of a term used in an earlier letter (page 47). Encourage dialogue; be sure students support their opinions. Then have them write their answers and a letter to "Wondering."

109

Even Though I Shouldn't . . .

Sometimes we do things that don't seem completely reasonable. We use the phrase "even though" to show that we know there are reasons why we shouldn't do what we have chosen to do. Look at the example below.

Even though it was past midnight, I decided to call my parents.

A. Write the letter of the phrase from the list on the right that best completes each sentence. Use each letter once only. The first one is done for you.

1. Even though I'm on a diet,   c

2. Even though I knew I had a test this morning,   ____

3. Even though I can't afford it,   ____

4. Even though I'm afraid of heights,   ____

5. Even though I might get fired,   ____

6. Even though I don't have a date,   ____

7. Even though I broke my leg,   ____

8. Even though I'm tired,   ____

9. Even though I felt well,   ____

10. Even though I've already seen that movie twice,   ____

a. I'm going to stay up a little longer.

b. I'm going to the prom.

c. I'm going to have some fudge.

d. I'm going to buy that expensive sweater.

e. I went to the doctor for a check up.

f. I'm going to Lori's birthday party.

g. I didn't study last night.

h. I'd like to see it again.

i. I took a chairlift to the top of the mountain.

j. I'm going to complain to the boss about this.

B. You can reverse the order of the phrases in a sentence using "even though," without changing the meaning of the sentence. Look at the example.

Even though I knew it was wrong, I read my sister's diary.
I read my sister's diary, even though I knew it was wrong.

Complete the following sentences with an "even though" phrase. The "even though" phrase should give an argument against doing the thing you have chosen to do. The first one is done for you.

1. I'm going to make supper, *even though I'm not hungry.* _____

2. I did my homework, _____

3. I'm taking a trip to Hawaii, _____

4. I'm going to wear my new suit, _____

5. I'm going to have a good time, _____

6. I took the money, _____

7. I wanted to watch the late night movie on TV, _____

_____

8. I voted for Tony Randolph, _____

Skill Objectives: Forming *even though* clauses; predicting outcomes. Read and discuss the introductory paragraph. When students show they understand the contradictory nature of *even though* sentences, assign Part A as independent work; later, have students read the complete (matched) sentences aloud. *Part B:* Allow time for students to share their different answers. You may wish to have students write more than one completer clause for each statement.

What Should He Have Done?

A. Tom went to Miami two weeks ago. He flew from Chicago and stayed for five days. He had a terrible time. Why did Tom have a terrible time?

1. He forgot to make a hotel reservation before he left. He had a hard time finding a room in a good hotel.

2. He packed only summer clothes because he thought Miami would be very warm. The temperature in Miami never went above 50°F that week.

3. He didn't take traveler's checks. His money was stolen from his hotel room.

4. He didn't lock the door of the car he had rented. Someone stole the car.

5. At the end of his vacation, he arrived at the airport too late. The plane for Chicago had already left.

What should Tom have done? Look at the list above and write five sentences. The first one is done for you.

1. *He should have made a hotel reservation before he left.*

2. _____

3. _____

4. _____

5. _____

B. Mike is a terrible mechanic because he can't follow directions. Yesterday, Jane took her car to Mike's Repair Shop. She gave Mike the list of directions below, but Mike didn't read the list carefully. Mike worked on the car for two hours, but he didn't do anything Jane asked. What did Mike do instead?

> *Jane's List*
> 1. Change the oil.
> 2. Fix the brakes.
> 3. Repair the window.
> 4. Install a muffler.

1. He changed the tires.
2. He fixed the clutch.
3. He repaired the door.
4. He installed a battery.

What should Mike have done? What shouldn't he have done? Write four pairs of sentences. The first one is done for you. Use it as a model.

1. *He should have changed the oil.*
    He shouldn't have changed the tires.

2. _____
    _____

3. _____
    _____

4. _____
    _____

Skill Objectives: Using past modals; problem solving. *Part A:* Read the anecdotal paragraphs aloud, and call attention to the sample answer; elicit that it goes with item 1 above, and review the structural change. Assign items 2 through 5. *Part B:* Follow the same procedure. Point out that each item requires two sentences, one positive and one negative. Review all answers for both parts orally when students have completed the page.

I Wonder Why

The four phrases below are often used to make statements and draw conclusions about past situations. Look at the chart below.

	Meaning	Example
MIGHT HAVE + past participle	it's possible	He might have seen it.
MUST HAVE + past participle	it seems certain	She must have gone home.
COULD HAVE + past participle	1) was (were) able to	They could have tried harder.
	2) it's possible	He could have gotten lost.
SHOULD HAVE + past participle	it was the right thing to do.	You should have called first.

A. Write a sentence responding to the following statements. Begin each sentence with one of the phrases from above. The first one is done for you.

1. Jim caught a cold last week, but he went skiing anyway. Now he's sick.
   He should have stayed home.

2. I wonder why Charles climbed in the window to his house last night.
   _____

3. Mr. Smith forgot to pay the oil bill last month. The oil company stopped delivering oil to his house.
   _____

4. I wonder why Jennifer didn't come to class all last week.
   _____

5. When I got up this morning and looked out the window, the streets looked wet.
   _____

6. My mother's birthday was yesterday. I forgot to buy her a present. She was disappointed.
   _____

Look at the three sentences below. Each has a slightly different meaning.

> I could have gotten up earlier. (I was able to.)
> I would have gotten up earlier. (I certainly would have.)
> I might have gotten up earlier. (Maybe I would have.)

B. Finish these sentences. Use *could have*, *would have*, or *might have*.

1. I'm sorry I didn't send you a post card from Miami. If I had known your address,
   _____

2. The weather was terrible on our vacation and no one went near the water. If the weather had been better, _____

3. John didn't study for the test. He flunked it. If he had studied for the test, _____
   _____

112

Skill Objectives: Using past modals; drawing conclusions. Review the meanings of the modals in the chart. *Part A:* Do the first three sentences orally, soliciting different answers for items 2 and 3. Then assign as written work. *Part B:* Be sure students understand the differences in meaning among *could*, *would*, and *might*. Do the three sentences orally, and encourage different answers. Then assign as written work.

If We Had Known . .

Read the two sentences below:

  If Susan had known about the party, she would have gone to it.
  If Tom had studied more, he might have passed the test.

These two sentences are in the past conditional. The past conditional is used to discuss things that could have happened, but didn't. The "If . . ." phrase uses the past perfect (*had known, had studied*); the other phrase uses *would have, could have,* or *might have* + a past participle.

Now answer these questions:

1. Did Susan go to the party? _____ Why or why not? _____

2. Did Tom pass the test? _____ Why or why not? _____

A. Read the story, then complete the sentences below. The first one is done for you.

Bob had planned to go to Europe. He wanted to visit France, Italy, Spain, and England. *But* the day before he was going to leave, he broke his leg and couldn't take his vacation. Poor Bob! Think of all he missed.

1. If Bob had gone to France, *he could have seen the Eiffel Tower.* ____

2. If he had gone to Italy, _____

3. If he had gone to Spain, _____

4. If he had gone to England, _____

5. If he hadn't broken his leg, _____

B. Write a past conditional sentence responding to each of the following situations. The first one is done for you. Use it as a model.

1. John didn't hear his alarm clock ring this morning. He got up late.
   If John had heard the alarm clock, he would have been on time.

2. I didn't have your address with me while I was on vacation. I couldn't send you a postcard.

   _____

3. I forgot to take my umbrella this morning. I got wet.

   _____

4. Sam and Sally had a terrible time on their vacation. The weather was rainy and cold and they couldn't go swimming, sailing, or water skiing.

   _____

   _____

Skill Objectives: Using past modals; understanding cause and effect; predicting outcomes. Discuss the time sequence of the first past perfect/conditional sentences. Ask what should have happened first; compare it with what actually did happen (in the students' opinions) in each sentence. Then have students look at the illustration, read the anecdotal paragraph, and complete Part A. *Part B:* Be sure students understand the instructions and the "done for you" sentence; then assign as written work.

What If?

A. You have learned about three different kinds of *if* clauses. **Use what you have learned to answer the following questions. Use the examples of each kind as a guide for writing your answers. Your answers may differ from other students'. That's all right. Just be sure they follow the pattern and make sense.**

Example: What will you do if your brother loses his glasses?
If my brother loses his glasses, I'll help him find them.

1. What will you do if the store is closed?

_____

2. What will you do if you hurt yourself?

_____

3. What will you do if it's hot tomorrow?

_____

4. What will you do if the phone rings?

_____

5. What will you do if you don't understand?

_____

6. What will you do if it rains?

_____

Example: What would you do if you forgot your notebook?
If I forgot my notebook, I would call my friend for the information.

7. What would you do if someone punched you in the nose?

_____

8. What would you do if your watch broke?

_____

9. What would you do if you were thirsty?

_____

10. What would you do if you were deaf?

_____

11. What would you do if you lost all your money?

_____

12. What would you do if you were a millionaire?

_____

Skill Objectives: Sequencing tenses with *if*; proposing possible solutions to problems. *Part A:* Review the sequence of tenses with *if*; call attention to the examples before items 1 and 7. Assign the page for independent work, then review answers orally.

Example: What would you have done if you had won the car?

If I had won the car, I would have screamed my head off!

13. What would you have done if you had seen the accident?

_____

14. What would you have done if you had burned your hand?

_____

15. What would you have done if you had left your keys in the car?

_____

16. What country would you have visited if you had planned the trip yourself?

_____

17. What would you have done if a mad dog had bitten you?

_____

18. What would you have done if you had missed the bus?

_____

B. Choose the correct form of the verb in parentheses and write it in the blank. The first one is done for you.

1. If John _____*has*_____ (have) enough money, he'll come with us.

2. If today _____ (be) Saturday, I would be home now.

3. If the weather _____ (be) nice yesterday, we would have gone swimming.

4. If I _____ (have) a million dollars, I'd take a trip around the world.

5. If John had gone to Paris last summer, he _____ (see) the Eiffel Tower.

6. If Americans _____ (exercise) more, they'd be in better physical condition.

7. If Mary _____ (get) up earlier, she wouldn't have missed the bus.

8. If Mary _____ (go) to Washington, D.C. she might see the president.

9. If you park next to a bus stop you _____ (get) a ticket.

10. If I were stuck in an elevator, I _____ (call) for help.

Skill Objectives: Sequencing tenses with *if*; proposing possible solutions to problems; completing sentences with correct verb form. Discuss the example sentence before item 13 in Part A. Then have students complete items 13-18. *Part B:* Do several items orally, then assign Part B for independent work. Check all answers orally with the class.

Reading the Newspaper: The Movies

The movies being shown in your area are usually listed in the newspaper. A schedule tells what films are playing at each theater, and what times the shows begin. Sometimes information is given about ticket prices or reduced prices for special days and early shows.

A. Read the movie schedule below, then answer the questions.

AVENUE THEATRE   816-6837
"FUNNY FACE" A. Hepburn/F. Astaire   3:45-8:00
"BREAKFAST AT TIFFANY'S" New Prints 1:30-5:45

ACADEMY CINEMAS 1-4-1296 Wash. St. 764-6060
HELD OVER BY POPULAR DEMAND!!
One of the year's most acclaimed
"4-star" rated comedies . . .
SHIRLEY VALENTINE
Starring PAULINE COLLINS and TOM CONTI
". . .Certainly one of the best movies of the year and
easily one of the best performances of the year. . ."
–D. Cunningham CBS-TV/NY
Shown at 2:10-4:45-7:20-9:55
"CRIMES & MISDEMEANORS"   5:00-7:40-9:35
"DRUGSTORE COWBOY"   2:15-4:45-7:15-9:15
Disney's "THE LITTLE MERMAID"
11-12-1-2-2:50-3:45-5:20-7-9
Cont. Mat. Daily $3.00 Until 6 P.M.

GALLERY THEATRES   672-0040
I. "★★★★ 'To Begin Again' Is Filled with Love."
–Jay Carr, Boston Globe,
of Academy Award Winner Best Foreign Film
"TO BEGIN AGAIN" (Volver A Empezar)
1:30-3:10-4:50-6:30-8:15-10:00
II. "★★★★ Carroll, New York Daily News
"Two hours of wonderful." Siegel, ABC-TV
STEEL MAGNOLIAS
2:30-5:00-7:30-10:00

COOLIDGE 1 & 2   934-2500
1. "THE TEN COMMANDMENTS"   2:30-7:00
In 70mm Stereo - Ends Thursday
2. "HUNGARIAN FAIRY TALE"
U.S. Premiere   2:20-4:10-6:00-7:50-9:40

1. Which film is probably in Spanish with English subtitles? _____

2. At which theater is a film being shown for the first time in the United States?

_____

What is the name of the film?

_____

3. How could you find out where the Coolidge Cinemas are located? _____

4. Which theater offers a double-feature) two movies in a row for the price of one)? _____

5. How long is the film *Shirley Valentine*? _____
About what time would the 9:55 show end? _____

6. How much would it cost for two people to go the 4:45 show of *Drugstore Cowboy*? _____ Do you think it would cost more or less to go to the 7:40 show? _____

B. How do you decide which movies to see? The Entertainment section often includes reviews written by movie critics. A critic describes the movie briefly, then gives his or her opinion about it. Of course, you will not always agree with the critic, but reading movie reviews often helps people choose films they will enjoy.

Read the review below, then answer the questions.

Can't Pay the Rent is the fourth film from director Zachary Christopher. With any luck at all, it will be his last. This alleged comedy is the story of a mild-mannered urban couple, Paul and Joanna Parkins, who rent the upstairs apartment of their home to a four-man rock band.

The few laughs that this film generates come from watching Joanna and Paul cope with the constant loud practice of the band. They wear earmuffs while dining by candlelight, and pantomime messages to one another over the rock-music roar. While some of this is funny, Paul's pantomime of the phone message, "Your brother has been hit by a car," is tasteless. It definitely isn't funny.

As for the "musicians," they are truly terrible. In the film, they are called "Make a Wish," and if mine had come true, the sound system would have broken down at the beginning of the first musical number.

To get the band out of the house, Paul becomes their manager. The ensuing nonsense and the unconvincing happy ending make this film totally unappealing. *Can't Pay the Rent* can't cut the mustard.

(Go on to the next page.)

Skill Objectives: Reading a schedule; making inferences; reading for main idea and details. Read the introductory paragraph. Let students study the movie schedule and then complete Part A independently. *Part B:* Have students read the introductory paragraph. Discuss what a *critic* is, and review the term *opinion*. Have students read the review. Discuss the questions at the top of page 117, help students understand *alleged* and *pantomime* through context. Then assign Part B as written work.

1. Did the critic like the film? _____ What sentence first tells you the critic's opinion?
_____

2. What does the critic mean by calling this film an "alleged comedy"?

_____

3. How do you "pantomime" a message? _____

4. What do you think happens at the end of this film? _____

_____

5. What does the final sentence of this review mean? Restate it in your own words.

_____

6. What is the tone (the writer's attitude or feelings) in this review?

    a. constructive and understanding   c. disappointed and very critical
    b. confused and unhappy   d. clever, witty, and humorous

C. Here is a review of the same film by a different critic.

Walk, run, jog, or drive, but hurry to the theater and see *Can't Pay the Rent.* This is the fourth and funniest of Zachary Christopher's films. He is clearly the latest Hollywood genius, and this film is going to ensure his reputation; it's going to be a blockbuster. It's the funniest movie that I have seen in years.

The story begins when Paul and Joanna Parkins rent their upstairs apartment to a rock group. The quiet couple get more than they bargained for with this noisy but excellent gang of musicians. Rather than hurt the band's feelings, however, the couple decide to cope with the noise and rowdiness that have taken over their peaceful home.

The scenes that show Paul and Joanna eating elegant dinners with earmuffs, or pantomiming telephone messages over the noise of the band, are howlingly funny. I haven't seen this kind of comic acting in years, and I wouldn't be surprised to see both Suzanne Winters as Joanna, and John Zimblast as Paul, receive Oscar nominations.

The hit musical group, Diamond, plays the band in the film. They are excellent, as always, and they sing their hit song, "Moonlighting," in the film. Between the laughs, the good music, and the happy ending, this is a perfect night's entertainment; you couldn't ask for more. I recommend this film highly. Go see it—tonight.

1. Did this critic like the film? _____

2. Discuss three things the two critics disagree about in their reviews. _____
_____
_____

3. Describe the one scene both critics agree was funny. _____

_____

4. What is the tone of this second review?

    a. enthusiastic   b. disappointed   c. surprised   d. comic

5. Do you think you would enjoy seeing *Can't Pay the Rent?* Why or why not?

_____

_____

Skill Objectives: Comparing and contrasting; establishing tone; reading for specific information. *Part C:* Have students read the second review and answer the questions about it. Then discuss the two reviews and their very different tones and opinions; reemphasize the difference between an opinion and a fact. Extension: Have students find reviews of movies they have seen (or bring in reviews of currently popular movies) and discuss the opinions of the class as compared to those of the critics.

117

Which Movie?

You can often tell something about a movie from its title. **Look at the movie schedule, then read the comments below.** All of these people were dissatisfied with the movies they saw. **Tell each person what movie he or she should have seen. Use complete sentences.** The first one is done for you.

CINEMA ONE Love in Rome	CINEMA TWO Invasion of the Extra-Terrestrials	CINEMA THREE Bonjour, Mon Ami
CINEMA FOUR Gunfight at Noon	CINEMA FIVE Laugh a Minute	CINEMA SIX Speedway 400
CINEMA SEVEN Happy Times, Happy Tunes	CINEMA EIGHT He Came to Help—The Roberto Clemente Story	CINEMA NINE The World at War

1. "I enjoyed *Speedway 400,* but I wish I had seen a comedy, something light and entertaining." *You should have seen* <u>Laugh a Minute</u>.

2. "We didn't enjoy *Love in Rome.* We would have preferred a real foreign film, something very European, with subtitles." _____

3. "*Invasion of the Extra-Terrestrials* was fine, but I wish I had seen something more serious and historical, something with some real information." _____

4. "*Gunfight at Noon* was silly. I wish I had seen a biographical picture." _____

5. "I liked *Happy Times, Happy Tunes* but my sons were bored. They like cowboy and adventure films." _____

6. "I didn't understand *Bonjour, Mon Ami.* I guess I should stick with my favorite kind of movie, American musicals." _____

7. "*The Roberto Clemente Story* was wonderful, but sad. I wish I had seen a light romance, a love story with a happy ending." _____

8. "*The World at War* was much too serious for me. I wish I had seen a car-race movie—something with a lot of action but no big problems." _____

9. "I didn't think *Laugh a Minute* was funny. I wish I had seen a science fiction movie full of hostile and scary space monsters." _____

Skill Objectives: Classifying; using past modals; making inferences; suggesting alternate solutions. Discuss categories of movies with the class. Be sure they know terms such as *musical, western, biography, foreign film,* etc. Discuss the nine movies listed and help the group decide which classification each one belongs to, making inferences from the titles. Discuss the answer to item 1, then assign the rest of the page for independent written work.

118

Find the Error (2)

There is a grammatical error in one of the underlined words or phrases in each sentence below. Find the error and circle it. Then correct the error in the blank under the sentence. The first one is done for you.

1. When the men finished (to paint) the house, they cleaned their brushes and went home.

   painting

2. Everyone agreed that if Tom would study for the chemistry test, he would have passed it easily.

   _____

3. Carla and Ron don't speak Hindi at all, and Ali doesn't neither.

   _____

4. Our university has the most tallest player in the league; he's over seven feet tall.

   _____

5. Even though I have seen that movie already, but I'd really like to see it again.

   _____

6. This book is one of the most excited that I have read in a long time.

   _____

7. One thing I admire about Susan is that she would rather reading a book than watch television.

   _____

8. Maria isn't sure yet, but she's thinking to going to the University of Chicago next year.

   _____

9. I'm furious with my mechanic; he repaired the brakes when he should of repaired the clutch.

   _____

10. When Americans go to Canada, they had better to carry a passport or some other official means of identification.

    _____

11. Our neighbor, Mr. Briggs, used to fat, but he went on a diet and lost a lot of weight.

    _____

12. If I won a million dollars, I will take a luxurious trip around the world with my best friend.

    _____

13. I felt sorry for my little brother last night; he was so tired to finish his homework.

    _____

14. Sara's tutor said that she will meet her downstairs in the cafeteria at 3:30.

    _____

15. I've done a lot of research, and it seems that a Cadillac is almost as expensive than a Lincoln Continental.

    _____

Skill Objectives: Finding and correcting grammatical errors; preparing for standardized tests. Review the format of this page (it is identical with that of page 78). Remind students that this is similar to items on some standardized tests that they may take in the future. Work through item 1 with the class and have them tell why "to paint" was circled and "painting" was written. Remind them that they must provide both kinds of answers in each item: circle the error and write the correction. Assign the page for independent work. Review all answers with the class, making sure students can find all answers and correct them.

Dear Dot

Dear Dot—

My parents flipped when they found out I went to an R-rated movie. (I am only fifteen.) They even threatened to go down to the movie theater and complain. Luckily, I talked them out of that. I would die if they made such a big fuss in public. Now they say that I have to tell them ahead of time what movie I'm going to see and I have to bring back the ticket stub to prove that I was at the correct theater. I think that they are making a mountain out of a molehill. The movie wasn't that different from what you see all the time on TV these days. How can I get Mom and Pop off my back?

Prisoner

Discuss each of the questions in class. Then write your answers.

1. What does "flipped" mean? _____

2. What does it mean if a film is rated "R"? _____
_____

3. What kind of person is Prisoner? The tone and language of the letter may give you some clues. _____
_____

4. Do you think Prisoner's parents' new rules are fair? Why or why not? _____
_____
_____

5. What does the expression "making a mountain out of a molehill" mean?
_____

6. Do you think that parents have the right to censor movies for their teenage children (decide which films their children are not allowed to see)? Why or why not? _____
_____
_____

Write About It

Now put yourself in Dot's place. Write a helpful answer to Prisoner. Remember, you want to help solve the problem, not make fun of the writer or criticize.

Dear Prisoner—

_____
_____
_____
_____
_____
_____

Skill Objectives: Reading for main idea and details; understanding figurative language; making judgments; expressing opinions in writing. Have students read the letter. Discuss each question in class. Encourage as much discussion as possible, but be sure opinions are supported. Then have students write answers to the questions. Suggest they use these answers as the basis for their letters. You may wish to assign the letter-writing activity as homework.

120

Vocabulary Review

Circle the word that does <u>not</u> belong.

1. tennis   soccer   skating   ping-pong
2. older   oldest   quieter   bigger
3. gentle   kind   nice   historic
4. heavy   curious   interested   nosy
5. similar   particular   alike   same
6. comics   editorials   chapters   classifieds
7. shy   bashful   complicated   quiet
8. bad   better   worst   worse
9. carefully   quickly   slowly   friendly
10. electrician   mechanic   economics   accountant
11. mountain   earthquake   tornado   hurricane
12. taken   wrote   flown   seen
13. New York   New Jersey   New England   New Mexico
14. past   present   progress   future
15. killed   murdered   assassinated   conquered
16. license   rules   regulations   laws
17. cattle   corn   potatoes   wheat
18. kitten   puppy   tiger   colt
19. yen   pound   ounce   rupee
20. immature   studious   childish   juvenile
21. one   four   five   seven
22. frightening   amusing   terrifying   horrifying
23. careful   confident   secure   self-assured
24. own   owe   possess   hold
25. fix   repair   adjust   retain
26. criticize   praise   admire   adore
27. central   main   important   middle
28. incredible   cautious   astonishing   amazing
29. verb   noun   question   adjective
30. march   rich   which   stomach

Vocabulary Review. Read the directions with the students and be sure they understand what they are to do. They may recognize this as the *Odd Man Out* activity. Do two or three examples with the students, then let them complete the page independently, reminding them that in this kind of exercise they must find the best answer, not just any possible one. When they have finished the page, review the answers, asking students to explain their choices.

Appendix: Parts of Speech

1. **Verbs** are usually action or thinking words. The verb is a main word in every sentence. Example: *drink, believe, live, go, know, call, run.*

   Auxiliary (helping) verbs help make a statement. Example: *am, is, do, don't, can, may, should, will.*

2. **Nouns** name a person, place, or thing. Example: *daughter, country, tree.*

   Proper nouns name a particular person, place, or thing. Example: *Tom, Ohio, English.*

3. **Adjectives** describe nouns. They tell what kind, how much, or how many. Examples: *lovely, blue, seven, several.*

   Demonstrative adjectives point out which one. Example: *this* book, *those* people.

   Possessive adjectives tell who it belongs to. Example: *her, our, my, their.*

4. **Adverbs** describe verbs. They tell how, where, when, and how often. Examples: *quickly, happily, very, today, there, sometimes, never, daily.*

5. **Prepositions** are small words that give directions. Example: *to, for, with, by, above, down, before, of.*

6. **Pronouns** take the place of nouns. Example: *I, you, he, she, it, him, us, them.*

   Indefinite pronouns. Example: *nobody, everyone, all, none.*

   Demonstrative pronouns: Example: *this, that, these, those.*

   Possessive pronouns: Example: *mine, hers, theirs.*

   Reflexive pronouns. Example: *himself, ourselves.*

   Relative pronouns. Example: *who, that, which.*

7. **Articles.** There are only three articles in English: *a, an, the.*

8. **Conjunctions** join two words or parts of a sentence together. Example: *and, but, if, so, or, although.*

What part of speech is the underlined word in each sentence? Write your answer on the line.

1. The cat <u>chased</u> the mouse. _____

2. My friends are coming <u>tomorrow</u>. _____

3. Your shoes are <u>under</u> the bed. _____

4. The <u>worst</u> day of my life was when I moved here. _____

5. <u>My</u> sister won the grand prize. _____

6. The girl cut <u>herself</u> on the broken glass. _____

7. We <u>could</u> visit your aunt. _____

8. That's a good <u>question</u>. _____

9. I heard <u>someone</u> come in. _____

10. <u>These</u> children are from Greece. _____

11. That's not <u>ours</u>. _____

12. I walked home <u>because</u> my bike had been stolen. _____

13. I left <u>it</u> at my house. _____

14. <u>Alaska</u> is the largest state. _____

15. A mechanic is someone <u>who</u> fixes cars. _____

16. <u>That</u> isn't fair! _____

17. The doctors performed <u>the</u> operation. _____

18. The Declaration of Independence was written <u>in</u> 1776. _____

Appendix: Parts of speech. Allow students time to review the parts of speech listed at the top of the page. Many students are unfamiliar with parts of speech even in their own language. Be prepared to complete the whole page as an oral exercise so that confused students can question and identify each underlined word. To challenge students more, have them copy the sentences on another piece of paper and label every word in each sentence with its correct part of speech.

End of Book Test: Completing Familiar Structures

A. Circle the best answer.

Example: Mary went to the library, but her friends _____.

a. weren't   (b. didn't)   c. aren't   d. don't

1. French _____ in Haiti.

   a. speaks   b. is speaking   c. is spoken   d. spoke

2. John has been playing soccer _____ 10:00 this morning.

   a. until   b. since   c. for   d. to

3. My sister is _____ getting married next year.

   a. thinking to   b. thinking for   c. thinking of   d. thinking in

4. Susan was _____ to go to work yesterday.

   a. very sick   b. too much sick   c. sick enough   d. too sick

5. My car _____ from the parking lot last night.

   a. is stealing   b. was stolen   c. has stolen   d. was stealing

6. Can you tell me where _____?

   a. lives Mary   b. does Mary live   c. Mary does live   d. Mary lives

7. I _____ stay home than go to a movie.

   a. would rather   b. would like   c. could   d. should

8. I always enjoy _____ swimming.

   a. going   b. to go   c. to going   d. go

9. The World Trade Center is _____ building in New York.

   a. the most high   b. too high   c. the most highest   d. the highest

10. My father _____ me stories when I was a child.

    a. was used to read   b. used to read   c. use to read   d. used to reading

11. Martha will be very happy if she _____ all her exams.

    a. will pass   b. passed   c. passes   d. is passed

12. She's done her homework, _____?

    a. isn't she   b. hasn't she   c. didn't she   d. wasn't she

13. If the weather had been nicer, May and Fred _____ swimming.

    a. should have gone   b. could have gone   c. went   d. have gone

14. Joe felt terrible yesterday because he _____ too much the night before.

    a. had eaten   b. has eaten   c. was eaten   d. had been eating

15. If I _____ you needed a car, I would've lent you mine.

    a. will know that   b. know that   c. had known that   d. have known that

End of Book Test: Completing familiar structures. The following pages will help you evaluate each student's strengths and weaknesses. Review directions and examples with the class, then assign the pages as independent work. Remind students to try each answer choice in the blank space to determine which choice is correct. Students should circle their answers.

123

End of Book Test: Completing Familiar Structures (continued)

16. If I made $18,000 a year, I _____ pay $3,000 in income tax.

    a. would   b. had to   c. used to   d. will

17. It's difficult to understand the teacher because she speaks _____.

    a. faster   b. very quick   c. very quickly   d. fastly

18. I wish that I _____ speak English well.

    a. could   b. would   c. should   d. might

19. I've never seen the movie "Animal House," and _____.

    a. either Joe has   b. neither has Joe   c. Joe hasn't neither   d. Joe has either

20. If Alice went to bed earlier, she _____ look so tired.

    a. wouldn't   b. couldn't   c. shouldn't   d. didn't use to

21. How many people _____ to your party?

    a. have you been invited   b. you have invited   c. have you invited

    d. have invited you

22. If you _____ to Washington, D.C., you might see the President.

    a. would go   b. go   c. will go   d. had gone

23. Since I've been in the United States, I _____ a lot of hamburgers.

    a. was eaten   b. should eat   c. have eaten   d. did eat

24. Robert had a bad headache last night and _____.

    a. so did I   b. I also had   c. so I had   d. neither did I

25. Janet and Lynn _____ go sailing because it was windy.

    a. weren't   b. may not   c. could not   d. would rather not

26. That car isn't _____ to drive.

    a. enough safe   b. safe neither   c. safe either   d. safe enough

27. Jim left class early because he _____ go to work.

    a. had to   b. would   c. would have gone   d. had

28. I've been getting bad grades on tests lately; I think I _____ study more.

    a. would   b. had   c. should   d. have

29. I don't know when _____.

    a. begins next semester   b. does next semester begin

    c. does begin next semester   d. next semester begins

30. The teacher _____ to write a composition.

    a. told to us   b. told us   c. said us   d. said to us

End of Book Test: Completing Familiar Structures (continued)

B. Read each sentence. Write the correct form of the verb on the line.

Example: Last night we _____heard_____ (hear) the President's speech on the radio.

1. Alexander Graham Bell _____ (invent) the telephone in 1898.

2. My cousin _____ (live) in Rome since 1980.

3. Wendy usually _____ (do) her laundry on Fridays.

4. I _____ (read) the newspaper when, suddenly, the lights went out.

5. A substitute teacher _____ (teach) our class yesterday.

6. My parents _____ (give) me a car for my birthday next year.

7. I _____ (be) a student for fourteen years.

8. The Statue of Liberty _____ (give) to the United States by France.

9. They said that they _____ (see) the movie twice already.

10. The Help Wanted ads _____ (find) in the Classified section.

Answer to puzzle on page 33

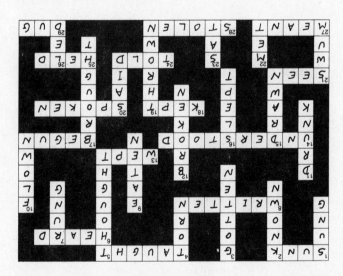

Answers to riddle on page 77, Section C

(1. Leo; 2. gold; 3. Pisces; 4. fits; 5. Take)

He got cold feet.

Answers to problems on page 84

8. 74, 96, 107, 81	4. 1125 yards
7. 89 seconds	3. $868.50
6. 70 miles	2. 200; 250; 305; 324
5. $53,200	1. 45

Answers to problems on page 96

4. a. $584; b. $7884	7. $5250
3. a. $480; b. $3520	6. $17.85 ($18.00)
2. a. $12.30; b. $94.30	5. $3136.50
1. a. $2.50; b. $52.50	

End of Book Test: Completing familiar structures (continued). Read the directions with the students. Call attention to the example and elicit that the past tense of the verb is required because of the clue *last night*.

125

End of Book Test: Reading Comprehension

Spaceships travel around the earth, go to the moon, and return home safely. The astronauts carry important supplies with them on the spaceship—food, water, and air. Sometimes there are problems on the spaceship, and the astronauts have to understand how the spaceship works in order to repair the problems.

In a way, all of us are really on a spaceship, the planet Earth. We move around the sun at 18 miles per second and never stop. On our spaceship we have four billion people and a limited supply of air, water, and land. These supplies, just like the limited supplies on the astronauts' spaceship, have to be used carefully because we can't buy new air, water, or land from anywhere else. Everyone needs air, water, and land to live—this is our environment.

The environment on our planet is a closed system; nothing new is ever added. Nature recycles its resources. Water, for example, evaporates and rises as invisible droplets to form clouds. This same water returns to the earth as rain or snow. The rain that falls today is actually the same water that fell on the dinosaurs 70 million years ago.

Today, the Earth is in trouble. Factories pour dirty water into our rivers. Many fish die and the water becomes unhealthy for people to drink. Cars and factories put poisons into the air and cause plants, animals, and people to get sick. People throw bottles and paper out of their car windows, and the roadside becomes covered with litter. Over the years, people have changed the environment. We have poured back into the land, air, and water more wastes than nature can clean. So we have pollution.

To continue to survive, we must learn how to use the Earth's resources wisely, without destroying them. We have to change our habits and stop dumping such enormous amounts of industrial waste into the water and air. To save the spaceship Earth, we must cooperate with nature and learn better ways to use, not abuse, our environment.

A. Circle the best answer.

1. The best title for this article would be _____.
   a. Water Pollution
   b. The Spaceship Earth
   c. Traveling in Space
   d. Problems of Astronauts

2. The population at present is approximately _____.
   a. four billion
   b. seventy million
   c. fourteen million
   d. fourteen billion

3. Which of the following is *NOT* an example of a recycled resource? _____
   a. air
   b. water
   c. cars
   d. land

4. Water is recycled _____.
   a. every million years
   b. from outside the atmosphere
   c. continually
   d. from other resources

5. The planet Earth travels around the sun at almost _____.
   a. 30 miles per second
   b. 70 miles per second
   c. 10 miles per second
   d. 20 miles per second

6. The author feels that _____.
   a. someday everyone will be an astronaut and live on a spaceship
   b. the earth will disappear when we have used up our resources
   c. trips to other planets will cause more pollution
   d. we must stop abusing the environment

End of Book Test: Reading Comprehension. Allow students ample time to read and reread the article and to answer the questions. The entire page is to be completed independently by the individual students.

B. Decide whether each of these statements is true or false. If it is true, circle the T. If it is false, circle the F.

T   F   1. Industrial waste is a type of pollution.

T   F   2. Dinosaurs lived seventy billion years ago.

T   F   3. Snow is an example of recycled water.

T   F   4. An empty bottle left in the woods is an example of litter.

T   F   5. Nature cleans all the wastes we pour back into it.

C. Finish these sentences

1. The author compares a spaceship to the planet Earth in this article because

_____

_____

2. To improve our environment we have to _____

_____

3. We have pollution because _____

_____

4. Two negative effects of water pollution are _____

_____

5. The word *recycle* means _____

_____

6. The word *litter* means _____

_____

7. The word *cooperate* means _____

_____

8. The word *abuse* means _____

_____

Skills Index

The pages listed below are those on which the skills are introduced and/or emphasized. Many of the skills appear, incidentally, on other pages as well.